The European Social Fund and the EU

The European Social Fund and the EU

Flexibility, Growth, Stability

Jacqueline Brine

SHEFFIELD ACADEMIC PRESS
A Continuum imprint
LONDON • NEW YORK

Copyright © 2002 Sheffield Academic Press
A Continuum imprint

Published by Sheffield Academic Press Ltd
The Tower Building, 11 York Road, London SE1 7NX
370 Lexington Avenue, New York NY 10017-6550

www.SheffieldAcademicPress.com
www.continuumbooks.com

British Library Cataloguing-in-Publication Data

A catalogue record for this book is available from the British Library

Typeset by Sheffield Academic Press
Printed on acid-free paper in Great Britain by MPG Books Ltd, Bodmin, Cornwall

ISBN   1-84127-128-4 (paperback)
          1-84127-409-7 (hardback)

Contents

Series Foreword

This is the eleventh book in the Contemporary European Studies series resulting from collaboration between the University Association of Contemporary European Studies (UACES) and Sheffield Academic Press. For over 30 years UACES has been the foremost British organization bringing together academics and practitioners interested in the study of contemporary Europe, particularly the institutions and policies of the European Union. Three years ago it was decided to launch this series to provide authoritative texts dealing with a wide range of important issues of interest to both those studying and teaching about European integration and professionals wishing to keep up with current developments.

Among the key objectives of the series were that it should reflect the broad range of academic disciplines involved in research on European integration and cover some of the policy areas that are rather neglected in the existing literature. This book by Jacqueline Brine is therefore a very welcome addition to the list, providing a sociological analysis of the development of the European Social Fund (ESF) based on her research experience in the field of education and training policy. She explores the way in which the discourse about the role of the ESF has changed over time and has reflected the evolution in assumptions about the nature of European integration itself and the purposes of social policy within it.

I am very grateful to Mike Newman, who has recently joined the editorial board, for providing editorial comment on the manuscript and to Heidi Robbins and her colleagues at Sheffield Academic Press for their professional expertise in ensuring that the book has been produced speedily and efficiently.

Jackie Gower
Series Editor

Acknowledgments

I am grateful to the following for the help given to me in researching and writing this book: the library staff at the University of Nottingham, especially the librarian in charge of the European Documentation Centre, and the counter staff and porters for finding and providing me with numerous dusty volumes of the *Official Journal*; colleagues at the School of Education, University of Sheffield for supporting me in my study leave so that I had the time to spend in Nottingham Library; Jude Marks, Jesse Marks, other family, friends and colleagues for the support they have provided in many different ways; to Julie Murray from Cedefop, John Field from the University of Warwick, and Mike Newman from the University of North London for their helpful comments on earlier drafts.

Abbreviations

Cedefop	European Centre for the Development of Vocational Training
CEEC	Central and Eastern European Countries
CoE	Council of Europe
CSF	Community Support Framework
CVTP	Common Vocational Training Policy
EC	European Community
ECSC	European Coal and Steel Community
EEC	European Economic Community
EFTA	European Free Trade Area
EIB	European Investment Bank
ERDF	European Regional Development Fund
ESF	European Social Fund
EU	European Union
GDP	gross domestic product
IGC	Intergovernmental Conference
MAI	Multilateral Agreement on Investment
NGO	non-governmental organization
NOW	New Opportunities for Women
NUTS	Nomenclature of Territorial Statistical Units
OECD	Organization for Economic Cooperation and Development
SEA	Single European Act
TEU	Treaty of the European Union
TNCs	transnational corporations
VET	vocational education and training
WIS	Women's Information Service
YfE	Youth for Europe

1 |

Searching for the Fund

A colleague asked me, why does the Social Fund matter?

It matters because, at the European level, it is a flexible instrument of policy and redistribution. Located at the interface of economic and social policies and framed by the dominant discourse of economic growth, it operates within a broad frame of reference to the labour market and the emergent European employment strategy. Moreover, framed by the equally dominant political discourse on the construction of the Union, and the sub-discourses of social cohesion and social exclusion, it redistributes resources to under-developed regions and to disadvantaged social groups. It matters because, at the Member State level, it makes a highly significant, but often barely visible, contribution to national vocational education and training (VET) programmes. For example, in the UK, despite, since the late 1970s, match-funding all government youth and adult unemployment training programmes, its existence has been barely acknowledged by either Conservative or Labour administrations (Brine 2002), for it not only provides the finance but the policy framework also.

I have previously explored differing aspects of the European Social Fund (ESF) at various points along its trajectory. Here, I step back to take a wider view of it as a major policy of the European Union.[1] There were three main reasons for wanting to do this: first, to consider the six reforms of the Fund in relation to each other, and to related social and economic policies and political changes; second, to consider the administration of the Fund in relation to policy-making and policy-management, and hence, the relationship between the Commission and

1. Within the introduction and concluding chapters reference to the EU is taken to imply the entire European project from 1957 onwards. However, the remaining chapters will reflect the actual usage of the time, that is, until 1967 the European Economic Community; from then until 1992 the European Community; and from 1992 the European Union.

the individual Member State; and third, to bring the Fund from the wings onto the centre-stage.

For many people working in the field of post-compulsory education and training, and that of regeneration, the ESF has been perhaps the most accessible and familiar face of the European Union. An elite group of administrators and practitioners within education, the voluntary sector and economic development have become expert in interpreting ESF guidelines and in successfully accessing the Fund; many others are baffled, confused and struggle to understand its constantly changing objectives and procedures.

The Fund has been seriously under-researched by academics. Within academic studies of the European Union it has often been overshadowed by more visible political debates and economic policies; within education, by national policies and debates. There has, however, been a steady stream of evaluation studies of individual projects, guides to good practice, guides on how to access the Fund, and Commission documents that outline the Fund's opportunities and past successes.

In a sense, its very obscurity is cause for concern. What purpose does it serve by this obscurity? Is there a relationship between obscurity and flexibility? Is it primarily a vehicle for redistribution or a proactive instrument of employment policy? Does it matter? These are the questions that lie behind the detailed exploration of ESF policy presented in this book.

While appreciative of the complexities of European policy-making that operate formally and informally (such as that detailed by, for example, Dinan 1999a, George 1996, Middlemas 1995, Richardson 1996, and Wallace and Wallace 1996), this book is based on the official policy texts that are freely available within the public domain, and which provide the basis for this discursive analysis of the Fund as both policy text and practice.

The argument of this analysis is that the flexibility of the Fund has enabled it to become both a proactive instrument of Commission policy and a significant redistributor of resources to support national policies. While the specific focus of its redistribution has changed to reflect the particular needs of the time (as for example, from social exclusion to social cohesion), the steady increase in Member State Fund management has coincided with its increased importance as an instrument of the European employment strategy. At the European level, the significance of the Fund lies first in its obscure or 'behind-the-scenes' effectiveness as an instrument of European policy, and secondly, in its visible effectiveness as an instrument of redistribution between Member States and regions. Yet paradoxically, at Member State level its effectiveness, particularly in the UK, is its invisibility as both an instrument of European policy and of European redistribution.

Introduction to the Social Fund

Economic growth and political stability between the Member States were among the driving forces behind the Treaty that established the European Economic Community (EEC) (CEC 1957). While the Social Fund's name suggests a home in social policy, (and indeed it has been housed in the Directorate for Social Affairs), its legal basis in the Treaty of Rome placed it in direct relation to the labour market.[2] These dual concerns of social and labour policy have existed from the beginning for 'the promotion of economic and social progress and the continuous improvement of living and working conditions ... [are] important aspects of European integration' (Beck *et al.* 1998: 57). Established through Article 123 of the Treaty, the ESF became operational in 1960. It was 'to improve opportunities of employment of workers in the Common Market and thus contribute to raising the standard of living'; it was to have the 'task of promoting within the Community employment facilities and the geographical and occupational mobility of workers' (CEC 1957, Article 123).

From an average 6% of the EC budget it had, by the mid-1980s, increased to 19%. By 2000, the Structural Funds represented the second largest redistributive instrument (following the Common Agricultural Policy), and moreover, 25% of Structural Fund resources were distributed through the Social Fund. Within the completion of the single market the Fund's role was further enhanced and, at that time, Springer (1992) foresaw a central role for it in providing a qualified and mobile workforce. By 2000, in the face of further enlargement, the Fund had become far more clearly a proactive instrument within European employment policy.

Since the original Treaty there have been six major reforms of the Social Fund.[3] The first reform in 1971 (CEC 1971a, b) began the shift in emphasis from retroactive redistribution to a more proactive approach

2.   Renamed in 1999 as the Directorate for Employment and Social Affairs.
3.   A summary detailing key legislation is provided in Appendix 1.

that gave the Commission a consolidating, coordinating and constructing role; negotiations of Commission/Member State control of the Fund continued throughout the subsequent reforms. The 1971 reform began the process of targeting the Fund onto specific social groups and occupational sectors.

The second reform of 1977 (CEC 1977a) continued to give Member States a greater administrative role and greater flexibility for incorporating the Fund into their national policies. At the same time the central coordinating and controlling role of the Commission was strengthened through the introduction of the Commission Guidelines that established the parameters for supported measures. In response to the emergent crisis of youth unemployment, the Fund was more tightly targeted onto these and other vulnerable social groups, and reference was made, for the first time, to the problem of structural unemployment. This highly significant reform not only continued the prioritization onto social groups but also onto those regions in greatest need of financial assistance.

The third reform of the Social Fund in 1983 (CEC 1983a) developed and strengthened the main concerns that were introduced in the 1977 reform. It increased its potential in national programmes and it targeted it more tightly onto particular social groups—especially young and adult unemployed people. The need to reduce regional imbalances was also an emerging matter of concern.

Following the Single European Act (CEC 1986b), the fourth reform (CEC 1988a) introduced a system of objectives into the Fund, and in doing so concentrated it first onto the regions of greatest need, and secondly onto long-term unemployed and young unemployed people. Preventative measures were introduced for the priority Objective 1 regions. In this way the Commission strengthened the Fund as a proactive instrument of European policy; at the same time, through the introduction of the Community Support Framework (CSF) it encouraged Member States to further incorporate the Fund into their national employment programmes.

The fifth reform of 1993 (CEC 1993a) continued the devolution of power from within a centralized framework. The objectives were redefined to place even greater emphasis on unemployment and exclusion from the labour market. The preventative measures that had been introduced into the fourth reform were extended under the new Objective 4 that covered the non-priority as well as priority areas. The most significant features of this reform, however, were the increased flexibility of the Fund; for example, the fundable measures were extended to include vocational guidance, counselling and basic skills and, immediately prior to the adoption of the concept of social exclusion, focused attention on the 'most disadvantaged' social groups.

Finally, the sixth and most significant reform since the second reform of 1977 was introduced in 1999 (CEC 1999a); it reduced the number of objectives to three and firmly targeted these onto the areas of greatest need; it became a key instrument in the European Employment Strategy (CEC 1999b). The range of fundable measures were extended and the Fund's flexibility considerably enhanced. In its strengthened guise as a proactive instrument of employment policies, it became a prominent contributor to Member State's national employment plans where the administrative, financial and managerial tasks and responsibilities were shared between the Commission and the Member States. Most importantly, the significance of the sixth reform lies in its enhanced intertwined capability as both a proactive instrument of European policy and its effectiveness as an instrument of regional (as compared to national) redistribution.

Across the six reforms from 1957 to 2000, the Fund became a more proactive instrument of employment policy. At differing times it was more, or less, focused on the regions of greatest need or on the most disadvantaged social groups. The tension between the Commission and the Member States persisted throughout and grew more important as, on one hand, the Commission tried to make the Fund as much a proactive instrument as possible and, on the other hand, the Member States wanted increased freedom to use the resources of the Fund as part of their own national strategies. The reforms of the Fund can be read as a tale of struggle between the Commission and the Member States with a sub-plot centred on the tension between national and sub-national agencies.[4]

Along with the focus on the Fund itself, the book considers its relationship to other European policies, six of which deserve an early mention. First, there was the obvious, yet messy, relationship with vocational training provided under Article 128 and the related Common Vocational Training Policy of 1963 (CEC 1963). In later years this

---

4. For example, John Field (1998) pointed out that Ireland was one of the more centralized Member States that the Commission focused on in its attempt to devolve part of the ESF budget and thereby give the sub-national authorities more of a stake in the European project.

relationship was strengthened through the Hanover Council's commitment to vocational training (CEC 1988b). Second, there was the relationship with education policy, from the early Janne Report (Council of Europe 1973) and Action Programme (CEC 1976a) to the European dimension in education (CEC 1988c) and the White Paper on education and training (CEC 1995a). Third, there was the Fund's relationship with broader social policy, from for example, the Social Action Programme of 1974 (CEC 1974a), to the 1989 *Charter of the Fundamental Social Rights of Workers* (CEC 1989a), to the 1994 White Paper on social policy (CEC 1994a). Fourth, there was the obvious relationship to employment policy, from the 1974 Directive on stability, growth and full employment (CEC 1974b), to the 1993 White Paper entitled *Growth, Competitiveness, Employment* (CEC 1993b), to the Luxembourg Council of 1997 (CEC 1997a), the employment chapter of the Amsterdam Treaty (CEC 1997b), and the European employment strategy (CEC 1999b). Fifth, there was the relationship with policy on youth, from an early concern with the vocational preparation for unemployed young people (CEC 1976b), to the 1988 action programme on Youth for Europe (CEC 1988d) and the concerns expressed in the 1995 White Paper on education and training (CEC 1995a). Finally, there was the relationship with equal opportunities policies. The Equal Opportunities Unit, established in 1976, exercised considerable influence over the Fund's provision for women (Brine 1995b, 1999b). The impact of each equal opportunities action programme can be traced within the Fund, the latest of which was the mainstreaming of equal opportunities throughout all EC policies and programmes (CEC 1994b). In addition to these six main areas of related policy, the relationship between the main objectives of the Fund and the 'Initiatives' was also an important means of developing the Commission's proactive agenda. These cross-EU programmes, centrally funded by a ring-fenced allocation and coordinated by the Commission, were introduced in the fourth reform of 1988 (CEC 1988a). The Social Fund is a large and clearly defined Structural Fund, yet it is, as will be seen throughout this book, strongly contextualized by these other areas of social policy.

Researching the Fund

There is a general lack of transparency around the Fund that is matched by the lack of theoretical and analytical attention focused on it. This may be directly related to its obscure location at the interface of more

highly visible policies such as those that fall under the gaze of econ-
omists, social theorists or educationalists. Even among those interested
in European policy, the Fund has been under-researched and under-
theorized—both in terms of policy-making and as an instrument of
vocational and employment policy. Despite its location in the Directorate for Employment and Social Affairs, it has generally been overlooked by both labour market and social policy theorists.

Collins (1983) produced one of the earliest, and subsequently few,
academic accounts of the Fund in which she provided a detailed history
of its development. Around the same time, Laffan published her much
referenced article (1983) in which she focused on the interaction
between European and national levels in the policy processes of the
ESF. Laffan found that the Fund operated in a policy vacuum where it
had little effect in directing national policies, but acted instead to complement national vocational training policies. She concluded that the
Fund was primarily an instrument of vocational training rather than an
instrument of employment policy, but predicted that increasing levels
of unemployment might lead to it becoming a meaningful employment
policy at Community level. Springer (1992), echoing Laffan, wrote that
for much of its history the Fund had played a minor role in employment
policies.

The Fund has been considered in varying degrees of depth by theorists of social policy, such as contributors to the edited works of Hine
and Kassim (1998), and Liebfried and Pierson (1995): for instance,
Anderson (1995), Jackman (1998) and Milner (1998). Studies on specific aspects of the Fund have included Macmillen's (1982) study of the
Fund's policy on migrants, and Moreton's (1992) study on people with
disabilities. More broadly, Hantrais (1995) has described the connec-
tions between its differing aspects—including education and training,
and compared this to the policy-making styles and objectives of the
national Member State governments. Falkner (1998) provides an
overview of the development of social policy and social policy-making,
and argues that it does not simply reflect the economic interests of the
Member State, but of the more complex interests of the policy community that has evolved. Geyer provided a succinct chapter in which he
asked if the Fund constituted EU regional policies, or was it perhaps a
bribe that keeps 'weaker Member States and interest groups committed
to the larger integration project' (Geyer 2000: 130). Geyer's interpretation is particularly relevant to this study for, pointing to the influence of

Robert Schuman on the development of the Structural Funds, he stated that this Fund could be used to help weaker Member States adjust to the new arrangements and help workers who might be threatened by them —two central themes that run throughout the following analysis. With these exceptions, however, the general lack of interest in education policy-making is compounded by the fact that there are very few educational researchers who are themselves interested in the European policy-making process (especially among those who publish in English).

Educationalists, relative newcomers to the study of European policy, have tended to concentrate on programmes such as Erasmus and Socrates that have directly affected higher education, or on comparative studies around specific issues and concerns (Teichler and Maiworm 1994; Corbett 1998; Osler 1998; Lindstrom 2000). Following the Treaty of the European Union (TEU) 1992, some educationalists have focused their attention on the European dimension of education or the role played by education in the development of European citizenship (Arnot 1997). Then there are those who evaluate the impact of policy, mainly through the funded programmes that accompany EC policy. Such studies are frequently, but not exclusively, comparative.

The Fund's original remit of training and retraining workers suggests that it would be of interest to those educationalists interested in vocational training. However, the European Centre for the Development of Vocational Training (Cedefop), for example, has concentrated on the non-ESF vocational training policies of Article 128, for the Fund itself is beyond its restricted brief.[5] Field (1994, 1998) is one educational researcher who has included the Fund within his studies where he found it to be a significant contributor to vocational training programmes. He also provides a welcome insight into the making of European education and training policy. See, for example, his discussion of the impact of the TEU on education and training, and, related to this, the designation of a new department, Education, Training and Youth[6] (Field 1998).

In my work I have considered the Fund's involvement in the construction of the EU (Brine 1995a), and its relationship to the discourse of equality and related equal opportunities policies (Brine 1998, 1999a). Earlier work (Brine 1992) was concerned with policy for unemployed

----

5.   Article 127 of the Treaty of Rome subsequently became Article 127 of the Treaty of Maastricht (TEU) and 150 of the Treaty of Amsterdam. See Appendix 3.
6.   Renamed in 1999 as the DG for Education and Culture.

and 'returning' women. Focusing on the policy process rather than policy-making itself, I have pursued two key strands: first, analysis of actual policy, such as that pursued in this book, and secondly, inter-pretation of policy by the UK government and other influential (regional or sectoral) intermediaries.

The policies and action programmes of the Equal Opportunities Unit have had a considerable influence on the Fund's policy discourse on women (Rees 1995), yet gender theorists have tended to concentrate on social policy issues such as pensions and maternity rights, or the development of equality law itself (Springer 1992; Prechal and Senden 1993; Mazey 1998). From within the field of political theorists, a few have made passing reference to the Fund, for example, Amin and Tom-maney (1995), Wallace and Wallace (1996), and Richardson (1996). Reference to the Fund can also be found in the work, primarily of political theorists, on the combined Structural Funds; see for example Burton and Smith (1996) and Staeck (1996), and also the work of Bache (1998) and Keating and Hooghe (1996) where they consider the related aspects of regional policy. Therefore, while the ESF may be relevant to many fields of study, it nevertheless has not been a central concern of any, and as such and with few exceptions has tended to fall through the gaps between disciplinary areas.

The policy-making process behind the Fund has also been under-researched, for whereas there are many political scientists who have focused on the policy-making process (for example, George 1996; Wallace and Wallace 1996; Cram 1997; Nugent 1999) the Fund has escaped their gaze. From among these political scientists there are those whose concern is the cohesiveness of policy characterized by shared dynamics. Then again there are other political scientists who see European policy as a mass of confusing, complex politics that change from issue to issue and level to level and are epitomized by those who refer to the 'garbage can' theory of policy (Richardson 1996). There are some who present a historical analysis of developments—the findings of which contribute to the contextual overview presented in each of the following chapters (Urwin 1995; Harryvan and van der Harst 1997; McAllister 1997). There are a small but growing number of sociologists and anthropologists who also have an interest in the European policy-making process. For example, McDonald (1997) provides an interesting study of identities among the Commission bureaucrats and the cabinet officials of individual Commissioners. Education and training policy, however, barely merits a mention in most of these often lengthy and complex works that tend to concentrate on the higher budget and apparently more glamorous fields, such as agricultural or economic policy.

While acknowledging the agency of Member States in making, interpreting and implementing policy (Anderson 1995; Brine 1999b), and of the influence of networks and experts (Middlemas 1995; Heinelt and Smith 1996; Peterson 1997), the focus of this book is entirely on the Fund at the European level, as a key policy instrument of the European project. In presenting a discursive analysis of the Fund, it is concerned with neither the actual policy making nor the policy implementation processes.

Discourse and Discourse Analysis

Discourse and discourse analysis have become significant features of social science research. Various attempts are made at categorizing the differing definitions and approaches taken by researchers. For instance, Titscher *et al.* (2000) details eleven such approaches. Howarth (2000) defines only four major categories. First are the positivists and empiricists who see discourses as frames or cognitive schemata, and the task of the analysis is to measure their effectiveness in bringing about certain ends. Second are the realists who see discourses as particular objects with their own properties and powers, and the aim of analysis is to unravel the conceptual elisions and confusions by which language enjoys its power. Third are the critical discourse analysts who, from within an overall sociological framework, see discourse as directly related to the social system within which it functions and with which human agency struggles. The task of the analyst here is to expose the relationship between discourse and power-relations. The fourth group are the post-structuralists and post-Marxists for whom discourse constitutes symbolic systems and social orders, and the task of the analyst is to examine their historical and political construction and functioning. The influence of Foucault is cited within both the critical discourse analysts and the post-structuralists. Whereas the demarcation lines of classification are contestable, the approach taken in this book is primarily a Foucauldian one that would be placed in the third category, the critical discourse analysis of the sociologists.

From within this perspective, discourse is a 'corpus of "statements" whose organisation is regular and systematic' (Kendall and Wickham

1999: 42). It is the linguistic and textual expression of ideas which, together with policies and social practice, constitute our subjective understandings of the world and our existence within it. While expressed linguistically and textually, however, discourse is neverthe-less distinct from language for it is embedded in the conditions of its production and its circulation; it is the way in which language is used—its accents and effects. It is 'politicized, power-bearing language employed to extend or defend the interests of its discursive community' (Fiske 1995: 3). Most significantly, discourses are not static or 'closed' but contain the possibility of innovation, are capable of change, and as such, reflect, and are of that time, constructed or produced differently. This flexibility is particularly true of dominant discourses, those that serve dominant power-related social and economic interests. Reflective of their time and their source of power, they are capable of considerable discursive change and flexibility, often absorbing and acting on com-peting and reverse discourses, while at the same time continuing to maintain their main power-related interests.

Furthermore, discourse, especially in its discursive practices, exists in an uneasy relationship to ideology and most particularly to the ideolo-gical intent that favours some and disadvantages others. The power of discourse to construct social subjectivities maintains ideologically deter-mined power differentials. However, discourse is more than simply the vehicle for maintaining ideological power relations. Levitas (1998) argues that discourse has a certain advantage over ideology in that it draws attention to the importance of language, not simply as a way of expressing the substance of that text, but also as that substance itself, and, wary of reducing material relations to discourse, it can, at its best, point to the power of the text while not excluding the power and reality of material forces.

The discursive analysis of the ESF is based on the official policy texts that are available within the public domain: the Treaties, Deci-sions and Regulations published in the *Official Journal* and key White Papers.[7] It is not in any way concerned with the 'behind-the-scenes' negotiations and compromises that led to that policy. Ball's (1994) assertion that policy exists both as text and as discourse, that it is a process and an outcome as well as a text, is pertinent here for it raises the question: 'to what extent can policy be read discursively, parti-cularly when separated from both its formation and its impact?' Despite

7.   See Appendix 2 for details of the legality of these documents.

being separated from the policy-*making* process, this analysis of the Fund is based on the actual textual outcome of that process for the textual representation of policy is an instrument of power that both expresses and constructs the European 'state' discourse; it has a legal effect on Member State national governments to which it is addressed and, moreover, it has a legal effect on the Commission bureaucracy who are charged with ensuring its implementation and evaluation. From within this tightly defined focus that excludes the negotiations between Commission bureaucrats, Commissioner's staff, Member State ministers and the influence of networks and experts (Middlemas 1995; Peterson 1997), there remains for analysis a significant amount of text related specifically or tangentially to the European Social Fund. As Henriques has written:

> The analysis regards every discourse as the result of a practice of production which is at once material, discursive and complex, always inscribed in relation to other practices of production of discourse. Every discourse is part of a discursive complex; it is locked in an intricate web of practices, bearing in mind that every practice is by definition both discursive and material (1984: 105-106).

I began the analysis of the Fund by identifying, locating and categorizing policy documents. I considered them in relation to the broader development of European policies and the construction of the Union. I then asked questions of the text itself: what exactly was the document saying; what was its essence; what made it different and what was its explicit aim? Next I considered the text discursively: what were the dominant discourses and what were the discursive shifts? The final step, explored most fully in Chapter 6, was to consider what Ball (1994) has termed the first and second order effects of policy. The first order are changes in structure or practice, such as its relationship to other European policies and to the construction of the Union. The second order are those effects related to social exclusion, opportunity and related aspects of social justice, such as the consideration, in Chapter 6, of the Fund as an instrument of redistribution to disadvantaged social groups and regions. The critical approach taken to this analysis of policy is one that, elaborated by Ozga (2000) intends not to present suggested reforms of the Fund, nor to provide solutions, but to contribute to our understanding—to theorize the Fund.

Although primarily a historic account, it is a Foucauldian one because it makes no assumption of progress, but as Kendall and

Wickham (1999) remind us, disturbs the taken-for-granted present. This is not a narrative of progress towards integration, but a thematic analysis located within the context of the dominant intertwined discourses of economic growth and political stability.

The Discourses of the European Union

Foucault's point (1980) that some discourses are 'dominant' and some 'reverse' is relevant to the 'dominant/reverse' status of discourses involved in the construction of the European Union (the fundamental political discourse). For example, within certain settings this political discourse is clearly dominant, yet in relation to a particular Member State, it can be seen as reverse. Some aspects of these discourses and those of the Member State overlap each other and some conflict. Where they overlap, as in their shared perspective on economic growth, they form an extremely strong dominant discourse, but where they conflict, as for example in their approach to social policy, then the EU discourse is in a reverse relationship to that of the Member State—or vice versa. Discourse is, then, fluid and messy, with a diverse range of interested, and, as in the case of the EU, conflicting parties contributing to its construction.

The analysis pursued throughout the remaining chapters of this book shows that the dominant political and economic discourses have, from their original intertwining in the Treaty of Rome, continued, albeit at different times in slightly different guises, to dominate the policies and practices of the EU. The detailed analysis provided in Chapters 2–5 chronicle the discursive shifts from their early dominance to the turn-of-the-century concerns expressed primarily through the sub-discourses of social cohesion, social exclusion, human resources and the pathologization of 'the unemployed'.

Although the economic and social needs of the Union are interlinked and the stability and well-being of each is dependent on the other, the political discourse has grown more important. It is concerned with inequality *within and across* the Member States—social exclusion. This sub-discourse of social exclusion presents a multi-deprivational model of inequality and disadvantage that purports to be based on social groups rather than individuals. The actual experience of social exclusion is variable and cushioned or compounded by numerous factors including those of gender, race, class, sexuality, disability and age.[8] It is also concerned with the national and regional imbalances of an enlarged Union—social cohesion.[9] This sub-discourse of social cohesion recognizes the material disparities that exist between the Member State and the regions of the Union.

Despite the location of exclusion and cohesion within the political discourse, these sub-discourses are nevertheless also linked to the dominant discourse of economic growth and the resulting processes of industrialization and urbanization—a process especially evident in the less-developed Member State and regions. From within the discourse of economic growth, industrialization has not only created wealth and an enlarged middle class but, at the same time, has generated social inequality, relative poverty and potential unrest—concerns of the discourse of political stability. Also located within the discourse of economic growth are the sub-discourses of human resources and the pathologization of the unemployed; the former with a relationship to social cohesion and the latter to social exclusion. The flows and contestations between these dominant and sub-discourses as they operate within the policy of the Fund are detailed in the following chapters.

Structure of the Book

I have structured the book with two, not necessarily distinct, readers in mind. First, for those interested in the development of the ESF over a particular period, in relation to a specific reform, or in its relationship to other key policy developments, a detailed policy analysis is given in Chapters 2–5. Secondly, for those readers interested in the shifts, the flow and the contestations of the discursive analysis of ESF policy, an overview of the discursive shifts of each period is given in the concluding sections of Chapters 2–5, and the main themes are then taken up again in Chapter 6. I have written the book so that it may be read in many ways, but in making each chapter independently coherent some repetition has been unavoidable.

Chapter 2 considers the years 1957–77, from the Treaty of Rome to the key second reform of the Fund (CEC 1977a). This was seen as a period of total focus on the worker and the labour market; unemploy-

8.   For further discussion of social exclusion within the EU, see Littlewood *et al.* (1999) and Atkinson and Davoudi (2000).
9.   For further discussion of social cohesion see Amin and Tommaney (1995).

ment was perceived as cyclical and policy was primarily concerned with the school to work transition period, or with retraining unemployed workers for a speedy re-entry to the market. It was also a period in which the Fund was targeted on specific groups of 'vulnerable' workers, such as agricultural and textile workers, and on specific social groups such as people with disabilities, older workers, young workers aged under 25 and women aged over 35. Both the political and economic discourses were dominant.

It was in the next period, 1978–88 (Chapter 3), that unemployment was perceived as structural, no longer limited to the young, and directly related to technological change. Other important policies of this time included the Single European Act (CEC 1986b), specific actions to *combat* unemployment (CEC 1982a, 1985a), and the arrival of the first action programme for equal opportunities between men and women (CEC 1982b). This period ended with the fourth reform (CEC 1988a) that introduced the priority system of objectives that targeted the Fund onto the areas of greatest need and the groups most vulnerable to long-term unemployment. The discourse of economic growth, expressed primarily through the sub-discourse of human resources was dominant and related to the political discourse on the construction of the EU, manifested as it was through the single market.

Chapter 4 covers the years 1989–96 and is focused on the emerging sub-discourse of social exclusion. The period began with the *Charter of the Fundamental Social Rights of Workers* (CEC 1989a) and included the Social Chapter within the TEU (CEC 1992a). At the same time, through the key White Papers of the period, 'social exclusion' was introduced as a major concern for the Union. The chief discursive tension during these years was between the sub-discourse of human resources and the emerging sub-discourse of social exclusion. The early rumblings of an emergent sub-discourse of pathologization are also discernible.

From 1997 onwards, the regions of the Union grew more important; social cohesion is the focus of Chapter 5. The two main themes of this period were first, employment (CEC 1997a) and second, enlargement (CEC 1997c). Whereas the dominant discourse of economic growth was still expressed primarily through the sub-discourse of human resources, the sub-discourse of social cohesion was strengthened and, reflecting the concerns of enlargement, was directly related to the overriding political discourse.

The concluding chapter (Chapter 6) draws together the themes and theoretical findings of the book. It explores the tensions that have surrounded the Fund and the related emergent and shifting discourses. From within the overall context of the dominant political and economic discourses, it focuses on the flexibility of the Fund as an instrument of labour market and VET policy, and as a flexible instrument of redistribution.

2 |

The ESF, the Labour Market and the Worker: 1957–1977

Political, Economic and Policy Context

This study of the European Social Fund begins in 1957 with the Treaty of Rome—the Treaty that established the European Economic Community (EEC) (CEC 1957). Urwin (1995), McAllister (1997), Harryvan and van der Harst (1997), and George (1996) all provide detailed accounts of both the period leading up to the Treaty and of subsequent developments in the construction of the Union. A major tension in these years surrounded the relationship between the Commission and the Member States and focused on Commission power and European interest as opposed to Member State sovereignty and national interest. The early hope by federalists was that the Commission would act as a catalyst for integration, but this did not happen: the role of the Commission was to draft and initiate the proposals that were then sent to the Council of Ministers. There was, therefore, a high level of Council control. Further understanding of the Commission–Member State struggle is evident in the remarks attributed to the first Community President, Walter Hallstein, who stated that the Commission's business was politics. This was interpreted by McAllister (1997) to mean that economic means were to be used to attain an essentially political goal. The tension between the dominant political and economic discourses were very apparent in the early years and continued to rumble, and sometimes erupt, throughout the rest of the century.

Harryvan and van der Harst (1997) argue that the Treaty itself and not the Commission was the main engine of integration, determining the direction of early policies. At the same time the Court of Justice had an important role in interpreting the Treaty and thereby influencing further developments. The European Parliamentary Assembly was not, in the early years, directly elected and furthermore, had very little authority. The EEC was, at that time, primarily an economic union that gave greatest consideration to the national interests of Member States. This was particularly evident in 1965 when, rejecting the proposed move towards majority voting, France refused to participate any further in European decision-making. This led to the six-month period dominated by the 'empty-chair' policy. Towards the end of this period, 1974, the Paris summit further strengthened the decision-making role of the Member States by establishing the European Council of Heads of State and government.

Economically, the years from 1958 to 1970 were ones of almost full employment for, supported by low-cost oil, the EEC was part of a post-war economic boom. Nevertheless, developing at this time were the multinationals that would subsequently grow stronger and make a central contribution to the development of economic, financial and cultural globalization. Most significantly in 1973, the Middle East oil crisis led six years later to a seismic impact on the EEC and other Western European countries. The period was one that shifted from the early years of economic ease and stability to the later years of economic threat, instability and rapidly growing globalization.

Politically, it was a period of conflict, compromise and consolidation. The six countries of Belgium, Netherlands, Luxembourg, Italy, France and the Federal Republic of Germany formed the EEC in 1957; two years later seven other European countries (Norway, Sweden, Finland, Portugal, Austria, Switzerland and the UK), formed a separate, purely economic group—the European Free Trade Association (EFTA). After only four years, however, the UK applied for membership of the EEC but was vetoed by France, and rejected once again in 1967. Finally, in 1973, in the first enlargement of the European Community (EC), the UK, Ireland and Denmark joined. In the intervening years, the Treaties of the European Coal and Steel Community (ECSC), the EEC and Euratom merged (1967) and became, officially, the European Communities—thereafter commonly referred to as the European Community; the customs union had been completed (1968), and the European Regional Development Fund (ERDF) had been established (1975).

Following the Treaty of 1957, a particularly noticeable political landmark was the Hague summit of 1969 where the French President, Georges Pompidou spoke of the need for completion, deepening and enlargement of the Community and a closer cooperation on external matters was agreed. Not only did the Hague summit effectively relaunch the Community, it also set it on track towards economic and monetary union and its first enlargement. Moreover, it finally provided the Commission with its own budget.

Despite the renewed impetus of the Hague summit and the 1973 enlargement, the 1970s are frequently described as years of inactivity— referred to by Harryvan and van der Harst (1997) as those of Europessimism, by McAllister (1997) as the locust years and by George (1996) as the dark ages. Nevertheless, the years immediately following the Hague summit of 1969 were ones in which shifts in policy were to have a lasting and significant effect on the future development of the Fund.

First, there was the reform in 1971 (CEC 1971a), where the Fund was shifted from being a retroactive instrument that, based on criteria determined by the Member States, had borne little relevance to European strategy, towards a proactive instrument that would be used to direct and implement a European Community-wide employment policy. Throughout this period the Fund was focused on the worker and the labour market. Attached to the first reform was a two-year budget that itself exceeded the total of the preceding years. This reform was a response to the acknowledged conceptual, financial and administrative shortcomings of the Fund in its original state—succinctly described by Taylor (1983) as 'too small, too slow, and lacking in a coherent strategy'. Second, there was the Social Action Programme of 1974 (CEC 1974a) that heralded a European social politic that, with a broader concern than simply that of the labour market, would address some of the negative effects of economic policy. Third, the establishment of the ERDF in 1975 confirmed the importance of a European regional policy. These regional and social concerns, along with an increased emphasis on the more proactive role of the Commission, were further developed within the second reform of the Fund in 1977 (CEC 1977a).

There were three key pieces of Social Fund policy during the 1957–77 period; these were the Treaty that established the EEC (CEC 1957); the first reform of the Fund (CEC 1971a, b), and the second reform (CEC 1977a). During this early period employment was assumed to be the norm, and any unemployment that existed was simply cyclical and related directly to the school-work transition period or, later, brief spells of unemployment in which the worker, after ESF-assisted re-training, would re-enter the labour market. As might be expected, the first 20 years in the life of the EEC were very important for later developments within the European Union. As previously stated, many of the policies still active at the turn of the century had their roots in policies introduced during the early years, for example the extensive youth VET policy that was first introduced through the Recommendation on vocational preparation for young people threatened by unemployment (CEC 1977b).

Treaty of Rome

The Treaty that established the EEC (CEC 1957) is a major document in the study of the ESF; it established the Fund and defined its limits. Articles 123–125 of the Treaty outlined the scope of the European Social Fund; Article 123 stated that:

> In order to improve opportunities of employment in workers in the Common Market and thus contribute to raising the standard of living, a European Social Fund shall hereby be established; it shall have the task of promoting within the Community employment facilities and the geographical and occupational mobility of workers.

The prime concern was the flexible worker, with employability and mobility a central feature of the Fund throughout this period; worker flexibility was Article 123's explicit aim. Although the Article referred to both geographical and occupational mobility, it was the latter which dominated policy, both in the years immediately following the Treaty and subsequently. Article 123 introduced the key European concept of the geographical mobility of workers; this was directly linked to the basic four freedoms of movement enshrined within the Treaty: the free movement of persons, services, goods and capital. However, in contrast to occupational mobility, the geographical mobility of Member State nationals remained generally under-realized.

Article 125 (sub-section 2) specified that funds could only be made available if it were impossible to re-employ unemployed workers in their old occupational area. Furthermore, it demanded that the re-trained person would work in a direct training-related occupation for six months following training. The demands for direct and relevant employment did not last beyond this early period.

Another notable article in the Treaty, related to vocational education and training, was Article 128. This laid down the principle for developing a Common Vocational Training Policy (CVTP) that until Maastricht was mostly concerned with the harmonization of Member State policy. Although separate from the Fund, the two frequently merged, especially as the Fund became a more proactive instrument of policy.

However, in relation to Article 123, despite the fact that the Treaty allowed for the Commission steerage, the pre-reform years were marked by the retroactive approach of the Fund; at that time the Commission acted as little more than a banker, reimbursing Member States for half of the training costs involved in getting people back into employment. Despite the proactive potential expressed in Article 123, the Council had a far more restrictive interpretation of the Fund (Collins 1975); each Member State established its own criteria for use. Geyer sums up this period by stating that 'the early ESF was a mixture of market-enhancing strategies, indirect redistribution and mechanisms for encouraging labour to view the common market strategy more positively' (Geyer 2000: 134). Consequently, those in the Commission who hoped for a more proactive Fund were frustrated by their lack of influence as the struggle for control of the Fund ensued between the Commission and the Council.

Common Vocational Training Policy: 1963

The dominant discourse of economic growth within the emergent European training policy was further strengthened by the very important Council Decision (CEC 1963), that, located in Article 128, laid down the Commission's general principles for implementing a common vocational training policy. Until the Treaty of the European Union (CEC 1992a) this Decision required the harmonization of vocational education and training policies. The discourse of economic growth was evident in the CVTP's demand that vocational training should contribute to a high level of employment. Member States were encouraged to use their economic policies to facilitate and adapt the skills of their labour force to the 'general economic situation and to changes in production technology' (p. 25). The Decision on CVTP laid down ten principles that collectively stressed the need for the Commission and Member States to cooperate, to harmonize policy, and to 'promote basic and advanced vocational training and retraining suitable for the various stages of working life' (p. 26). Echoing the Treaty of Rome's Article 123, the fourth principle provided for Commission activities that would promote 'the geographical and occupational mobility of workers within the Community' (p. 26), and the ninth principle prophetically stressed the relevance of training to the 'situations caused by economic expansion or recession, technological and structural changes' (pp. 27-28). In the early 1960s, the dominant discourse of economic growth became increasingly linked to the fundamental political discourse on the construction of the EEC. The two most significant features of the combined discourse were the harmonization of VET policy, and the need for VET to address the labour market consequences of global and European restructuring. At this time, the Commission was arguing that the ESF should also be used to develop a common vocational training policy (Collins 1975).

First Reform of the ESF: 1971

The first reform of the ESF (CEC 1971a) began the process of turning the Fund into a more proactive instrument of employment policy and in doing so established the notion of a European-wide strategy and individual Member State responsibility for structural changes in the labour market—structural changes brought about by the emergent global economy, by the predicted new technological changes in production and by the construction of the European Community itself. The budget of the first two years of the reformed Fund exceeded the total of the preceding 12 years. From within this major change in emphasis, the reform made several other notable amendments to the Fund.

First, and most significantly, it introduced a system of 'priorities and guidelines' through which funding for specified social groups and selected sectors was to be prioritized. This significant and long-lasting change in the Fund reflected the tenth principle of the CVTP; that is, the need to pay particular attention to the special problems concerning specific sectors of activity, or specific categories of persons. Article 5 of the reform referred specifically to 'the absorption and reabsorption into active employment of the disabled, and of older workers, women and young workers' (CEC 1971a: 53). Although the Regulation that implemented the reform (CEC 1971b), referred to workers difficult to place 'on account of their age', it specifically defined eligible women as those aged over 35 and young workers as those aged under 25, but it stated firmly that this did not include the 'initial training of young people immediately after completion of their term of compulsory schooling' (p. 926). The reform Regulation also provided assistance for 'handicapped persons who may be able to pursue a professional or trade activity after medical rehabilitation, vocational training or retraining' (p. 925). Most significantly in relation to the existing dominant discourse of economic growth, the Regulation made the first direct reference, within the Fund, to the social consequences of economic practices: 'long-term structural unemployment and underemployment [was] widespread in some areas of the Community' (CEC 1971b: 924)—an early reference to the theme that was to dominate Social Fund policy for the next 30 years. It also added that it was 'necessary to promote the training of highly skilled manpower'—a far less consistent theme.

A further four significant developments arose from the 1971 reform (CEC 1971a, b): the mobility of workers; targeting the Fund onto specific social groups; strengthening administrative procedures; and the concern for migrant workers. A further Regulation (CEC 1971c) reinforced Article 123's statement regarding the geographical and occupational mobility of workers: the Fund would enable workers 'to adapt their qualifications, to agree to change their place of work and residence and to avail themselves of the most suitable opportunities for using their professional knowledge' (CEC 1971c: 929). This additional Regulation went on to specify the numerous practical ways in which this aid could be applied, for example in paying housing costs, or the travel and resettlement expenses of trainers and trainees. A couple of years later, a further related Regulation (CEC 1973a) specified the allowances available for three groups of persons who might leave their homes in search of work: the unemployed (man), the young unemployed person and the elderly worker undergoing locational retraining.

The second significant development from the 1971 reform was that the Fund was targeted onto particular occupational workers and specific social groups: agricultural or textile workers, migrant workers, 'handicapped persons' and unemployed young people. In 1972 a Council Decision (CEC 1972a) focused the Fund onto 'persons leaving agriculture to pursue non-agricultural activities'; this concern was directly related to the discourse of economic growth and most particularly to the common agricultural policy which dominated the Commission at that time. This Decision further stated that 'the imbalance of employment recorded in the agricultural sector is such as to necessitate a considerable number of workers changing employment and thus having to acquire new qualifications and sometimes moving their homes' (CEC 1972a: 73). A central feature of the Fund at that time was the belief that unemployed people would move across the Community in search of work.

Again, reflecting the direct relationship of the Fund to the dominant discourse of economic growth yet another Decision (CEC 1972b) focused attention onto textile workers. It stated that the 'imbalance' that led to 'a considerable number of workers [needing] to change their employment ... will continue in future years and is in danger of becoming more marked following the progressive opening up of markets following the special measures adopted in the context of the commercial policy of the Community' (CEC 1972b: 75)—that is, the move towards the common market. Four years later a subsequent Decision (CEC 1976c) noted, in obscure 'Eurospeak', that the textile sector continued 'to be affected by quantitative and qualitative imbalances' and accordingly that particular action of the Fund was prolonged.

The Decisions on both agricultural and textile workers stressed that the Fund should 're-direct' workers towards self-employment, for, according to the Council Decision referred to above, (CEC 1972a), this was thought to be 'most suited to the mentality and abilities of persons who have worked in agriculture' (CEC 1972a: 73), and similarly so for self-employed textile workers. The Commission's interest in self-employment was also addressed to 'handicapped' persons (CEC 1971d). Self-employment was reiterated in the subsequent Council Decision (CEC 1974c) on ESF 'action for handicapped persons' which otherwise concentrated on 'good practice' and training trainers.

The final key Decision relating to the 1971 reform was that which targeted the Fund onto young unemployed people aged under 25 (CEC 1975a)—a concern that was to increase and then remain a highly significant feature of the Fund during the following decades. This particular Decision was itself a direct consequence of the Social Action Programme (CEC 1974a) considered below. The process of targeting the Fund onto specific occupational groups was subsequently discarded, whereas that of targeting it onto disadvantaged social groups continued throughout the rest of the century as more groups were identified as suffering the social consequences of economic growth, and hence being in need of additional support.

The third significant development related in part to the Commission's concern with yet another social group—migrant workers. It was important not simply because of its focus on migrants, but more for the fact that it blurred or extended the Fund's competency. The Regulation (CEC 1974d) stated that:

in order to facilitate the reception and integration of migrant workers and members of their families into their social and working environment, provision should be made for an aid to assist the children of migrant workers to adjust to their new educational environment' (CEC 1974d: 1).

This Regulation was the first to address itself to education, and more specifically, to the education of children—that is, almost 20 years before the TEU and the competency for the European dimension in education.

Finally, the fourth development related to the Commission's enhanced role in Social Fund policy, that of strengthened administrative procedures. The 1971 reform required Member States to draw up an approved list of those public bodies deemed eligible to access it, and the subsequent Regulation (CEC 1972c) tied them into the operation of the Fund. They were each to act as a responsible gate-keeper and go-between between the Commission and the public body, ensuring that correct procedures were followed and that the required audit information would be freely and readily available for Commission inspection. Inevitably, there were difficulties, particularly in the ability of Member States to gain Commission approval for projects before actually beginning them—a complete turn-around from the pre-reform retroactive system. A further Council Decision (CEC 1973b), temporarily extended the deadline for proposals provided they were 'submitted to the Commission prior to carrying out the operation'. The early confusions surrounding submission dates, the delays in payments and the tangled mess of Member State and Commission bureaucracy continued to haunt the operation of the Social Fund throughout the twentieth century. The confusions were compounded by the continued fine-tuning of the 1971 reform as, for instance, in the Regulation (CEC 1973a) that specified the actual amounts of assistance given to encourage occupational mobility. Following an extension (CEC 1973b) a series of Commission Decisions throughout 1973 granted separate assistance to each Member State for what were frequently referred to as 'retraining and resettlement operations'.

The prime concerns of mobility, proactive prioritization of Fund actions, education, and Member State administrative responsibility, were all either introduced or considerably strengthened by the 1971 reform, and each became a major theme in the future development of the Fund and in the construction of the Union.

The ESF and Education Policy

The years between the first and second reforms (CEC 1971a, b) of the ESF were the pivotal ones in which social and education policy was introduced. In 1973 the Council of Europe[1] published the Janne Report on the educational needs of the 16–19 age group (Council of Europe 1973). I include it here because, while not a Commission document, it nevertheless raised key concerns that are subsequently developed through Commission policy. The Janne Report examined both the sociological and the pedagogical aspects of the 16–19 age group which it defined functionally as: 'the age at which the young person is initiated into membership of society as a whole and into the "roles" which that membership involves' (p. 13).

The Janne Report introduced several new concepts that can be traced forward within the policies of the EC: lifelong learning, guidance and counselling, and educational equal opportunities. The report recommended re-thinking education provision for this age group and suggested a process of 'deschooling' so that these years would become the beginning of *permanent education:* 'The education of the 16 to 19 age group needs to be thought out afresh, not in traditional terms as the final phase of school life, but rather as the first phase of permanent education' (p. 18). Over the following decades this notion of permanent education developed into the central educational concept of lifelong learning.

A second emphasis in this report was that of guidance and counselling—an approach which was subsequently integrated into all policies relating to the education and training of youth and, within the ESF, (especially objective 3),[2] to youth and adult unemployment. The Janne Report defined guidance and counselling as an individual approach as opposed to orientation which it saw as group based. It stressed,

1.   The Council of Europe (CoE) is quite distinct from the European Council referred to throughout the remainder of the book. Like the EEC and EFTA the CoE emerged out of the aftermath of the Second World War with a particular brief to establish a consultative assembly elected by national parliaments, to draft a European charter of human rights and to establish a court that would enforce its decisions. Membership of the CoE includes non-EU and EU states; at the beginning of the twenty-first century there are 41 members.

2.   The priority system of objectives, introduced through the fourth reform of 1988 (CEC 1988a), is described in Chapter 3.

however, that both approaches were equally concerned with giving young people knowledge of the choices that were available to them.

A third area of concern to receive early attention in this report was that of equality of educational opportunity. Drawing on the reports of the member countries, the report acknowledged some improvement in equality of access but pointed out that disparity of outcomes continued. It considered three aspects of educational inequality: social class, the 'sex factor' and the 'regional factor', and concluded that an increasingly heterogeneous population had rejected the previous homogeneous male middle-class values of the educational systems. In its early recognition of the diverse needs of the population—by social groups, gender and region, the Council of Europe's Janne Report echoed the 1971 reform of the ESF.

Education for young people should, the report suggested, integrate general and vocational education, it should incorporate the latest educational technology (at that time, audio-visual media), and it should be interdisciplinary and taught by teachers who themselves undergo regular retraining; education provision for young people should be more radical and more flexible. Reflecting the general understanding of the time that youth unemployment was simply cyclical and related only to the school–work transition state, the Janne Report made only passing reference to unemployment, for this was not, at that time, a matter for further consideration.

Two years after the Janne Report, the European Commission published its first Action Programme in the field of education (CEC 1976a). Given the absence of legal competency within the field of compulsory education the programme concentrated on the important founding principle of mobility—of staff, students and researchers; on cooperation in higher education, and on the importance of languages. The Education Action Programme also referred to the educational dimension of the 1974 Social Action Programme (CEC 1974a), specifically the educational needs of children of nationals of other Member States. Shifting the scope of educational activity away from its vocational basis within the discourse of economic growth, the Action Programme stressed that education was not simply related to economic concerns but that 'education is central to the full and healthy development of the Community' (CEC 1976a: 1).

Following on from the suggestions of the Janne Report and the Education Action Programme, the 1976 Resolution (CEC 1976b) concerning the preparation of young people for the transition from education to working life, continued to emphasize guidance and counselling as well as the need for vocational preparation within the final years of compulsory schooling. It also picked up on the Janne Report's concern for equality of educational opportunity, particularly that of girls, young migrants and the 'physically and mentally handicapped'.

It is, however, the subsequent Recommendation (CEC 1977b) on vocational preparation for young people threatened by unemployment, that was related most closely to the European Social Fund and to the earlier Decision of 1975 (CEC 1975a) that had first referred to the particular needs of unemployed young people. This latest 1977 Recommendation stated, in the first of a long line of constantly rising statistics, that the 'level of youth unemployment [had] more than doubled since 1973' so that in the spring of 1977 there were, in the European Community, approximately two million unemployed young people aged under 25, and that furthermore, it would actually grow more acute. It predicted that unemployment would therefore remain a serious *socio-economic* problem and that to solve the unemployment problems of young people, wide-ranging action would be needed: 'economic policy, education policy, labour-market policy' (CEC 1997b: 18). It also pointed out that those with 'the greatest difficulty in finding jobs [were] often those who ... benefited least from what the school system was able to offer' (p. 20). Echoing the comments of the Janne Report the Recommendation on vocational preparation remarked that those who left school at the minimum school leaving age did so because they found the 'school atmosphere uncongenial and unresponsive to their adolescent interests' (CEC 1977b: 20).

Although this Recommendation on vocational preparation (CEC 1977b) identified three groups of vulnerable young people (girls, young migrants and the disabled), it concentrated its efforts on those unemployed and insecurely employed young people who had never received vocational training. Those who had previously received training (whether employed or unemployed) were not included in this action. Referring to the previous year's Council Directive on equal treatment for men and women (CEC 1976d), the Recommendation stated that it applied 'with equal force to young men and young women without discrimination' (CEC 1977b: 19).

Education policy was, like ESF policy, not simply a statement of broad intention, but a policy that provided considerable detail with regard to the curriculum and, accompanied as it was by actual funds, provoked further policy change. For example, the Recommendation on vocational preparation (CEC 1977b) provided for training in basic literacy, numeracy and social skills, in understanding the basic principles of economic and social organization, and for practical initial training in a broad skills area. It stressed the need for vocational guidance, for co-operation with employers and social partners, and for allowances sufficient to cover maintenance, fees and the incidental costs of courses. The payment of such allowances continued to be a significant aspect of European training policy, especially with regard to what would become the sub-discourse of social exclusion.

The concerns of early education policy—permanent education, guidance and counselling, equal opportunities, the inclusion of 'new' technology, and geographical and occupational mobility—all became important features of the Social Fund. Equally important, within early education policy there was a recognition of its potential role in addressing the social consequences of economic growth and the construction of the European Community.

The ESF and Social Policy

Early European education policy is directly related to the pivotal Social Action Programme of 1974 (CEC 1974a). This first piece of social policy came midway between the 1971 and the 1977 reforms. The Council Resolution on social action had its roots in the critical meeting of Heads of State that was held two years earlier in Paris (October 1972); the Heads of State had recognized that economic expansion was not an end in itself, but one that should lead to an improved quality of life, and as such, as much importance should be attached 'to vigorous action in the social field as to the achievement of Economic and Monetary Union' (CEC 1974a: 1). The Heads of State invited the Commission to draw up a social action programme and thereby began the interest in social policy that was to lead, 20 years later, to the Social Chapter of the Treaty of the European Union (CEC 1992a). The Paris summit made three further key decisions: first, they pointed to the future relationship between the Social Fund and social policy, and stated that it was the Fund that would provide the much-needed resources for the social action programme; the role of the Fund would therefore be strengthened. Second, it agreed to the first regional fund—

the European Regional Development Fund (ERDF) that, established in 1975, strengthened the emergent sub-discourse of social cohesion. Third, it consolidated the decision-making role of Member States by establishing the European Council of Heads of State and Government.

There were three main sections to the Social Policy Action Programme (CEC 1974a): first, the attainment of full and better employment in the Community; second, the improvement of living and working conditions; and third, the increased involvement of management and labour in the economic and social decisions of the Community. In addition to reference to the Fund, the Social Action Programme also sited itself in relation to Article 128, from which it stressed the need to implement a common vocational training policy especially in relation to training standards. It stated its intention to set up a European Centre for the Development of Vocational Training—subsequently established in 1975 and known by its French acronym, Cedefop (CEC 1975b). In common with the emergent themes of this period the Social Action Programme made clear its intention to 'take action for the purpose of achieving equality between men and women as regards access to employment and vocational training' (CEC 1974a: 2), and to 'initiate a programme for the vocational and social integration of handicapped persons' (p. 2). Similarly, the concern with migrant workers, the free movement of workers, the young and the aged worker, was also present, although priority was given to migrant workers, gender equality, a common vocational training policy and the establishment of Cedefop.

The other major pieces of social policy at this time were the pilot schemes and studies set up by the Council Decision to combat poverty (CEC 1975c), which it defined as that which affected individuals or families whose resources (i.e. goods, cash or services), were 'so small as to exclude them from the minimum acceptable way of life of the Member State in which they live' (CEC 1975c: 34). This early policy on poverty paved the way for the future Council Decision on action to combat poverty (CEC 1985b) and the Council Resolution on combating social exclusion (CEC 1989b).

Second Reform of the ESF: The 1977 Regulation

The 1977 Regulation consolidated the individual actions framed by the developing social policy of the preceding six years and introduced the second reform of the Fund (CEC 1977a). In order to manage the Fund 'more rationally' it transferred more of its administration onto the

Member States, thereby enabling it to be more easily incorporated into national employment and training policies. Unlike the extensive freedom of the early transition years, however, it further strengthened the concept of *Guidelines* which, published by the Commission, defined the framework and the prioritization of Funds within which the Member State was to operate. The Regulation stated that:

> the guidelines shall be geared to the economic and social situation in the Community. They shall take account, with a view to ensuring the harmonious development of the Community, of the extent of the imbalances in the labour market and the economic capacity available for correcting them (CEC 1977a: 3).

This meant that at the same time as the Member State was given more administrative responsibility the Fund itself became a far more proactive instrument of Commission policy.

Equally significantly, the Regulation focused the Fund even more closely onto the training needs of unemployed people. As the impact of the 1973 oil crisis began to hit the Western capitalist states, so this Regulation made the first Commission policy reference to the now overly familiar concept of *structural unemployment*. The Regulation stated that it would fund operations that

> are directed towards eliminating long-term structural unemployment or under-employment, for the benefit of persons who are unemployed or who would become so after a specific period, or those who are under-employed or have had to cease pursuing an activity as a self-employed person (CEC 1977a: 2).

Continuing the principle of prioritization begun in the 1971 reform, the 1977 reform stated that, 'as a matter of priority', 60% of the Fund was to be reserved 'for operations which are aimed at eliminating long-term structural unemployment or under-employment' in specified regions (p. 2). In this way the reform reinforced the regional concerns expressed within the ERDF and introduced, as a major feature of the Fund, the critical concept of regional prioritization as expressed through the emergent sub-discourse of social cohesion. At the same time the second reform continued to prioritize specific social groups: 'handicapped' persons, those who needed to update their occupational knowledge, workers aged 50 and over, and young people unable to find work either because of their lack of qualifications or because of lack of demand for the qualifications they possessed.

On the same day that the Council adopted this Regulation (CEC 1977a), several further Regulations and Decisions were published that added the finer detail and closed some existing gaps; the Fund was targeted far more closely onto 'disadvantaged' social groups and under-developed regions—especially those 'regions characterized by an especially serious and prolonged imbalance in employment' (CEC 1977c: 7; CEC 1977d); the pre-1977 Decisions on agricultural and textile workers were updated (CEC 1977e). Geographical and occupational mobility also continued post-1977: for instance, a Council Decision (CEC 1977f) reaffirmed the Fund's assistance to migrants and, as previously, the children of migrants; moreover, it focused on the particular training needs of those welfare workers and teachers who ran integration courses for both the migrant workers and their children.

A further Decision (CEC 1977g) of the same date focused on the training needs of women; it referred to the meeting of the Heads of State in Rome during March 1977, and their agreed need for action related to the training and employment of women. The Heads of State had concluded that 'vocational training for women must be accompanied by complementary measures' (CEC 1977g: 14)—measures such as reimbursement of childminding costs were to have a positive impact on women's training (Brine 1999c). The age of eligibility was lowered from that originally set by the 1971 reform (35 years), so that women aged over 25 with no, or insufficient, qualifications became eligible for ESF assistance. Despite the lowered age qualification, however, eligibility was only extended to those women who were unemployed or wanting to enter or return to the labour market after a long break such as that spent in caring for their children.[3] This Decision also stated that Funded measures must prepare women for working life, motivate 'new choices of occupation' or 'facilitate entry into occupations where there [were] job prospects' (CEC 1997g: 14).[4]

The following year a further post-reform Decision (CEC 1978a) tightened up the administrative procedures between the Commission and the Member State, especially in relation to submission dates and payments. A few months later a new Regulation (CEC 1978b) introduced

3.   Anderson (1995) points out that the beneficiaries of the Fund are only those who are 'eligible'—it is not an entitlement.

4.   See Brine (1999b) for further discussion of the Equal Opportunities Unit and its relationship to the ESF.

'job creation' into the Fund. The aim of this was to promote the recruit-ment or employment of young people under 25 years of age, either through the creation of additional jobs or through the creation of projects for the creation of additional jobs. The Fund's assistance for job creation did not, however, cover jobs created by the state, or by public authorities.

The second reform (CEC 1977a) and its subsequent early amendments provoked a critical discursive shift away from the early dominance of the discourse of economic growth towards the developing sub-discourse of social cohesion. For the first time, the Fund now targeted particular regions—regions that were seen to be 'disadvantaged' by either economic policies or by the construction of the EEC itself. To this end, it was more tightly targeted and, despite the apparent greater involvement of the Member States, was 'guided' and ultimately con-trolled by the Commission. At the same time, the Fund continued to target specific social groups; in addition to the existing young and 'handicapped' people were those vulnerable to changes in production, those aged over 50 and women aged over 25. Most significantly, for the first time, the Fund referred to the problem of structural unemployment and introduced the concept of job creation. Here were the beginnings of an emergent sub-discourse of social exclusion.

Discursive Shifts

The two dominant discourses within the Treaty of Rome were those of economic growth and the political stability underpinning the construc-tion of the EEC, and, as expected at this time, the two were intricately related. In the immediate post-World War II period, the economic need to rebuild the European economy and provide employment was linked with the need to construct and maintain peace between the previously warring nations, and to construct cohesion against East European communist states. The need to develop the European economy and to create high employment was directly linked to the need for economic, social and political stability. The Fund's concern with occupational mobility reflected the envisaged changes in production, caused at that time more by the change from war to peace than by the newly emergent technologies. It is in this indirect relationship of the economic discourse to the social and political stability of the European Community that the Fund was, even at that early stage, linked to the dominant political discourse and the emergent sub-discourse of social cohesion, and to a lesser extent, social exclusion. Within the dominant discourse of economic growth and therein linked to the sub-discourse of human resources, a discourse of the flexible worker emerged: a dominant post-Fordist discourse of the late century. In the early 1960s, alongside the harmonizing pursuit of a common vocational training policy, the dominant discourse of economic growth was clearly linked to the fundamental political discourse on the construction of the European Community.

From within these notable discursive shifts, the overriding themes within this chapter were first, the control of the Fund: this was expressed through the tension that existed between the Commission and the Member States regarding the extent to which the Fund was a retroactive or proactive instrument. The second theme was that centred on the worker and the labour market. However, although there was as much concern with the worker at the end of the period as there had been at the beginning, there were notable changes. The early concern had been with the employability and the mobility of workers—a sub-discourse of human resources and its emergent variable—that of the 'flexible' worker—flexible in a post-Fordist sense rather than in terms of geographical mobility. Another early concern had focused on the need to establish the notion of state responsibility for structural changes in the labour market, changes caused by changing production from a war footing to that of peace and from the impact of the construction of the European Economic Community. Acknowledgment of the structural changes caused by the 'new' technological impact on production came only towards the end of this period.

These concerns were clearly located within the dominant discourse of economic growth, intricately linked with the need to construct a European Community that had a strong economic and trading base. Yet, the Community was to be more than just a free trading area, and the need for peace and cooperation between the Member States was equally strong. The political discourse of the construction of the Community was also a central feature of the early years, particularly in relation to the concept of harmonization of Member State policy, to the central consolidating and constructing role of the Commission, and to its struggle with the Member States. From within the political discourse, concern for social and political stability formed a discursive bridge between the early dominance of the discourse of economic growth and the emergent sub-discourses of social exclusion and social cohesion. It is at this discursive intersection that European social policy grew, and where the Fund was subsequently found, balanced between the two.

3 |

The ESF, Technological Change and 'the Unemployed': 1978–1988

Political, Economic and Policy Context

The early struggle for supranationalism was discarded as the European Community entered a period of reduced activity and consolidation; the decision-making powers of the Heads of State were consolidated and the process of majority voting was agreed for those matters concerning the single market.

These years were, in the first instance, dominated by the move towards the single market. The 1985 White Paper on the internal market (CEC 1985c) was followed one year later by the Single European Act (SEA) (CEC 1986b) that began the process that would lead to its completion by the end of 1992. The SEA created the legal and political basis for the subsequent transformation of the Structural Funds (CEC 1988e) and focused attention on the need for economic and social cohesion.

The second area of importance was the further enlargement of the Community: Greece joined in 1981, Spain and Portugal in 1986. By comparison with the majority of states already in the Community, these three were far less economically developed; moreover, following several national elections in 1981 there developed a political tension between the centre-left governments of the south and the varying shades of centre-right governments in the north. Nevertheless, the Franco-German core of the Community remained strong and was further strengthened by the arrival, in 1985, of Jacques Delors as the new Commission President. Delors, fully supported by the French President Mitterrand, was to have considerable impact on the future development of Community policies. The political tension between the Commission and the Member States was expressed in terms of federalism versus neo-liberalism and was predominately centred on Delors for the Commission against Margaret Thatcher for the UK Government.

The third significant development began in 1979 with the establishment of the European monetary system. This was followed by the London Council of 1981, at which the Genscher–Colombo plan for an Act of European Union was presented and, as McAllister (1997) notes, was coolly received. Subsequently 'watered-down' by the Solemn Declaration of Stuttgart (CEC 1983b), this eventually led to the Treaty of the European Union (CEC 1992a).

While less contentious than the previous period, the three centrally important ambitions introduced during these years dominated the peripheral policies of the time. These were the single market, monetary union and the construction of the Union itself. To quote McAllister, in this 'strange period ... beneath an unpromising surface, things were beginning to move ... quite a lot of spadework had been done by those with ambitious agendas' (1997: 160-61).

Economically, the years between 1978 and 1988 were critical. The traditional industries of steel and shipbuilding were in definite decline; the opportunities offered by the new technologies were yet to be realized—it was, at that time, predominately a threat to many sectors and numerous occupations. The economic powers of Japan and the United States were another growing threat, but most important was the effect of the 1973 oil crisis, which was subsequently compounded by a second oil crisis of 1981. McAllister quotes the Commission as stating that 'after the 1973 oil crisis [the Commission had] sucked itself dry by stepping in over and over again to cushion the effects of the quadrupling oil prices' (McAllister 1997: 133).

This, then, was a pivotal period in which economic globalization, technological changes in production, demographic change and the advent of the European single market all impacted on the labour market and, consequently, policy makers were faced with the problem of structural unemployment and changing skill needs. The decline in heavy manufacturing industry led to large numbers of unemployed older male workers. At the same time, the new technological industries and the burgeoning service industries attracted female part-time workers. This was the period commonly seen as one in which Europe changed from a Fordist economy to a post-Fordist one.[1] Throughout the 1980s the Commission produced a continual stream of reports that each detailed the likely impact of either new technology or the single market upon a

---

1.   Arguments in favour of a neo-Fordist reading are given in Brine 1999b.

particular occupational sector or social group (see for example, CEC 1985d; 1986a; 1987a)

The policies of the time that impacted on the Social Fund were first and foremost those related to unemployment, as for example, the Resolution that detailed the guidelines for a Community labour market policy (CEC 1980) and the Resolution on action to combat unemployment (CEC 1982a). Particular concern was focused on the unemployment of young people, for instance the 1982 Resolution to improve the preparation of young people for work and to facilitate their transition from education to working life (CEC 1982b), and the Decision of 1987 that introduced an action programme for the vocational training of young people (CEC 1987b). Linked to the fundamental concern over rising unemployment were general vocational training activities such as the Resolution of 1993 that covered the relationship between training and the new information technologies (CEC 1983c), and the Decision of 1985 on the comparability of vocational education and training qualifications (CEC 1985e).

The second major area of policy that affected the Fund was that concerning the equal opportunities of women and men. The Commission's Equal Opportunities Unit, rooted in Article 119 and established in 1976, produced in 1982 the first Equal Opportunities Action Programme (CEC 1982c). This was followed by the Recommendation on positive action for women (CEC 1984), and then by the second Action Programme that covered the years 1986–90 (CEC 1985f). The impact on the Fund of both the unemployment and the equal opportunities policies are explored below.

Specifically with regard to the Fund itself, there were two key pieces of ESF policy during this period—the 1983 Regulation of the third reform (CEC 1983a), and the 1988 Regulation of the fourth (CEC 1988a). The late 1970s and early 1980s were still dominated by the major second reform (CEC 1977a) discussed in the previous chapter. As stated above, the Single European Act (CEC 1986b) laid the legal ground for the critical Regulation of 1988 that combined the Structural Funds and thereby set the parameters for the Social Fund itself (CEC 1988e).

In the previous period, the policy emphasis was clearly located on the worker; however, in this period, although the worker was still present, there was an increasing concern for the *unemployed* worker—female as well as male. There were two major factors behind this new interest in the woman worker. First, it reflected the changing labour demands referred to above, and second, it responded to the new Equal Opportunities programmes.

The next section of this chapter is focused on the central concern of unemployment with particular attention paid to those policies related to vocational training in general and the Social Fund in particular. This is followed by a consideration of the impact of the Single European Act upon the Fund. The third reform of the ESF (CEC 1983a) is the focus of the next section. An exploration of the impact of equal opportunities is then provided, and subsequently continued within Chapter 4. The analysis of the following section is focused on the fourth reform of the Fund (CEC 1988a). The chapter concludes with an analysis of the discursive shifts that took place between 1978 and 1988.

The ESF and Unemployment

During this period the general concern with unemployment was expressed primarily through a series of Council Resolutions that were eventually to lead to the White Paper on growth, competitiveness, and employment (CEC 1993b) discussed in the following chapter. This section is focused on the employment Resolutions that were most significant for the future development of the Fund.

In 1980 the Council agreed a Resolution (CEC 1980) in which they detailed their guidelines for a Community labour market policy, emphasized the growing need for active labour market policies and called upon the Commission to take initiatives to comply with it. In its preamble the Resolution pointed to several causal factors: economic and demographic changes and trends, Community enlargement, new technologies, changes in the international economy and structural adjustments resulting from the 1973 oil crisis. It concluded that:

> the employment situation is likely to continue to give cause for concern in the years ahead, particularly in certain regions of the Community ... [and it is therefore necessary to achieve] an employment policy at national and Community level which will reinforce the fight against unemployment (CEC 1980: 1).

Labour market policy was to be effected 'by making consistent and full use of vocational guidance, training and retraining and placement'; the chief means of Community assistance was to be through the Social Fund which, it asserted, 'constitutes an important instrument for the implementation of labour market policy' (p. 1).

The Resolution listed seven areas of action: knowledge of the labour market; vocational guidance, training and retraining; placement; a forward-looking approach; measures on behalf of specific categories of workers; regional measures and sectoral measures. In this way the Resolution introduced two new concerns that, over the coming 20 years, were to become increasingly important: first, the need for knowledge of the labour market, especially at a local level; and second, an emphasis on vocational guidance that was to grow in importance alongside rising unemployment. The Resolution pointed to the importance of vocational guidance for young people, for job-seekers and for those whose employment was threatened. Finally, training was also seen as a means of implementing equal opportunities for men and women.

The Council, in the employment Resolution, reiterated its support for three other foci that had originated, or had been confirmed, in the second reform (CEC 1977a): first, the general trend that allowed Member States to use the Fund in support of national training policies; second, the targeting of provision onto particular social groups (social exclusion); and third, yet to a far lesser extent, the recognition of particular 'disadvantaged regions' (social cohesion). In referring to particular social groups the Resolution pointed to 'individual categories of job-seekers who encounter particular problems on the labour market', and it specified 'young people, women, elderly, migrant and handicapped workers' (CEC 1980: 3). Furthermore, it added: 'special attention should be given to employment problems resulting from lack of or insufficient qualifications, long-term unemployment and maternity' (p. 4). The Resolution was centred on the needs of particular social groups and although reference was made to regional disadvantage, it was only a secondary concern. Located on social groups, the emergent sub-discourse of social exclusion remained, at this time, dominant over the secondary regional concerns of social cohesion.

As part of a developing general framework to combat unemployment, the Council, two years later in the 1982 Resolution, reiterated its 'grave concern at the persistently high level of unemployment particularly among young people' (CEC 1982a: 1), and added that attention should be given to those regions most affected. In requesting the Commission to present proposals, the Council presented a far more proactive approach to unemployment. It pointed out that industrial restructuring programmes should pay attention to employment problems, that the potential of small and medium-sized enterprises should be explored, that job-creation opportunities should be considered, and that priority should be given to the vocational training of young people.

Also, in 1982, a further Council Resolution referred to the need to improve the preparation of young people for work and the need to facilitate their transition from education to working life (CEC 1982b). The Fund would be targeted onto the most disadvantaged sections of young people through pilot projects that would be part of national strategies—measures designed to get young people out of school and into work experience, and employers and trade unionists into schools to work with the young people there. Information and guidance was to be given to people aged 14–18.

This Resolution led five years later to the Decision that established Petra, the Action Programme for the vocational training of young people and their preparation for adult and working life (CEC 1987b). The inclusion of 'adult' as well as 'working' life appeared to acknowledge that training would not necessarily lead to employment. Most importantly, this Decision sowed the seeds for the future pathologization of young people, particularly with regard to their alleged lack of social skills. The Decision's main concern was to provide a European dimension to the Member State's own policy measures and training initiatives; they were to do their 'utmost to ensure … that all young people in the Community who so [wished, would] receive one year's, or if possible, two or more year's, vocational training in addition to their full-time compulsory education' (CEC 1987b: 32). Finally, the Decision drew attention to the particular needs of young people who were most at risk—the disabled, disadvantaged and those who left school with few or no qualifications.

There was, throughout the period, a great deal of Council and Commission activity around the key problem of unemployment, especially concerning young people. Although it was still possible to discern a sub-discourse of social cohesion, the emergent sub-discourse of social exclusion was far more prevalent, and introduced themes that were subsequently to grow more important: the focus on youth, on the particular needs of those with no or few qualifications, and on guidance as an employment measure.

The Single European Act

The Single European Act of 1986 (CEC 1986b) followed the White Paper on the internal market (CEC 1985c) and established a single market where goods, services, capital and labour would move freely. Following the years of comparative inactivity the SEA (along with the arrival, in 1985, of Jacques Delors as Commission President), represented a new hope for those who wanted a federal Europe. The SEA was significant for the development of the Social Fund for two main reasons: first, it paved the way for the 1998 reform of the Structural Funds (CEC 1988e), and second, it introduced, through Article 130, the competency on economic and social cohesion.

The SEA added a new title to Part 3 of the Treaty of Rome—title V, economic and social cohesion—and through Article 130, entitled the Community to 'develop and pursue its actions leading to the strengthening of its economic and social cohesion':

> the Community shall aim at reducing disparities between the various regions and the backwardness of the least-favoured regions (CEC 1986b: 13).

The Act consolidated the reference made in the second reform (CEC 1977a) that the Fund would contribute to economic and social cohesion, and it demanded from the Commission a comprehensive proposal on the ways in which the Fund would be amended in order to meet the new demands, and the ways in which it would be coordinated with the other strands of the Structural Fund. The pivotal discursive location of the Social Fund, sited as it then was between economic growth and political stability as evidenced in the emergent sub-discourse of social cohesion, was clearly evident in the Act's amendment of the Treaty.

Following the SEA, two years later the European Council met in Hanover (CEC 1988b) and considered the issues involved in the progress towards the completion of the single market. The Council considered the social aspects of the single market and stated that 'the achievement of the large market must go hand in hand with improved access to vocational training, including training linked with work, in all the Member States' (CEC 1988b: 165). The Council thereby reinforced its commitment to vocational training and to its significance within the single market.

Third Reform of the ESF: The 1983 Regulation

The previous chapter concluded its analysis of the second reform (CEC 1977a) by referring to the Regulation adopted in 1978 (CEC 1978b) that drew attention to the 'growing scarcity of jobs available to young workers under 25 years of age' and hence allowed the Fund to be used in the creation of additional jobs, provided such jobs were not created by the state or other public authority. This 1978 youth Regulation illustrated the overlap between the pre-existing dominant discourse of economic growth and the early rumblings of what would become the sub-discourse of social exclusion. Two years later, a further Regulation (CEC 1985g) extended this job creation strand to include the creation of jobs for non-professional self-employed persons aged over 25. The second reform's concern with particular social groups continued, not only with regard to unemployed young people but also towards others who suffered from employment 'imbalances'.

The third major reform of the Fund was adopted in 1983 (CEC 1983a) and it increased the Fund's proactive role by targeting it even more specifically onto vulnerable social groups and, following an additional Regulation (CEC 1977c), onto specified regions also. In this way the reform attempted to have an impact on both the groups and regions seen as most vulnerable to the economic and political changes of that time: the sub-discourses of social exclusion and social cohesion were thus being constructed. From within the emergent sub-discourse of social exclusion, the Fund redistributed resources towards disadvantaged groups; provided trainee incomes, trainer training, accommodation and travelling expenses and, for people with physical disabilities, the adaptation of the workplace. The reform reiterated the possibilities of job creation for unemployed young people and extended eligibility to include additional jobs which fulfilled a 'public need' provided they were 'giving access to the labour market and facilitating employment in a stable job' (CEC 1983a: 1). There remained, in the early 1980s, the belief that training, especially for the young, would, and should, lead to stable employment. The considerable material support of the reform was, however, fairly short-lived, for as unemployment increased so the particular high function of the Fund decreased.

At the same time, from within the emergent sub-discourse of social cohesion, it provided, for the first time, an increased rate of assistance to particular disadvantaged regions: the French overseas departments, Greece, Greenland, Ireland, the Mezzogiorno and Northern Ireland. Within the subsequent Decision (CEC 1983d), Article 5 provided 60% of eligible expenditure to projects within these regions—as compared to the 50% for projects in all other regions—a Member State public body supplied the remainder.

The 1983 Decision was important for several reasons: first, it focused the Fund onto vulnerable groups, especially the young; second, it reiterated the possibility of the Fund's contribution to Member State labour market policies; and third, it removed the Treaty's requirement that training should lead to employment. In targeting the Fund onto vulnerable groups, the third reform Decision stated that the Fund,

> as an instrument of employment policy must ... contribute as effectively and as consistently as possible to the solution of the most serious problems and in particular the fight against unemployment, including structural underemployment and the promotion of employment among the groups most affected (CEC 1983d: 38).

Article 4 listed the other vulnerable groups as unemployed people, women wishing to return to work, 'handicapped' people, and migrant workers. The sub-discourse of social exclusion, not yet explicit, was being strengthened. There is, in this Decision, as part of a definite proactive approach, a steady construction of the sub-discourses of both social cohesion and social exclusion.

Nevertheless, despite the wide definition of 'vulnerable groups', the Decision stated that 'a significant part of the Fund's resources must be allocated to measures in favour of youth employment' (CEC 1983d: 38). Reinforcing the second reform (CEC 1977a) the Decision reiterated that the Fund should contribute to national labour market policies, particularly those that were focused on young people. In complete contrast to the first reform (CEC 1971a) where the Fund was not intended for the initial training of school-leavers, this 1983 Decision reversed that ruling for it declared that:

> These operations shall include in particular those intended to improve employment opportunities for young people, notably by means of vocational training measures after completion of full-time compulsory schooling (CEC 1983d: 39).

In this particular respect the second and third reforms reflected the changing dynamic between the Commission and the Member States. As the Commission gained more control of the Fund in order to use it as an instrument of Community employment strategy, it remained, at the same time, flexible enough for Member States to use as part of their own national strategy. Moreover, the practical financial impact of the Fund should not be overlooked; for example, in the UK the ESF match-funded the government's entire youth and adult unemployment training programmes. The change in school-leaver eligibility reflected the rapidly rising youth unemployment that faced policy makers both at Commission and Member State level.

Third, the 1983 Decision removed the Treaty's requirement that training should lead to employment. Article 125 of the Treaty of Rome had demanded that a retrained person would work in a direct training-related occupation for at least six months following their training. This was a highly significant shift in policy intention that reflected the difficulties of achieving this within a labour market that was dominated by changing production, rising unemployment, and the creation of the single market. This shift was a major factor in the developing sub-discourse of social exclusion and the pathologization of unemployed people—the demand that training be related to employment was removed from the trainers and placed on the individual trainee.

The ESF and Equal Opportunities

Along with concerns regarding unemployment, the need to address the employment and training implications of new technology, and the implications of the single market, the fourth major influence on the Social Fund during this period was the emerging discourse of equal opportunities. The first reform had referred specifically to the 'absorption and reabsorption into active employment of ... women' (CEC 1971a: 53). The related Regulation (CEC 1971b) stated that only those women aged over 35 were to be eligible for Fund support. As part of a series of Decisions that followed the second reform of the Fund (CEC 1977a), the age of eligibility was lowered to 25—provided the women were unemployed, wanted to enter or return to the labour market, and had no or insufficient qualifications. The Decision of the second reform also stated that Funded measures were to prepare women for working life, to motivate 'new choices of occupation' or 'facilitate entry into occupations where there [were] job prospects' (CEC 1977g: 14).

The Commission's Women's Information Service (WIS) provided an interpretation of the second reform:

> The highest priority is given to programmes that train women for occupations that have been traditionally reserved for men or for programmes that train them for new jobs open to both sexes. When first priority applications have been met, second priority is given to programmes that concern traditional female employment but (i) are for women involved in

mass dismissals; (ii) *or* facilitate women to reach a higher level of
employment than their previous employment (CEC 1981: 2).

While this interpretation gave equally high priority to both training in
traditional male occupations and to new jobs, training related to
hierarchical under-representation was far down the list. The overriding
significance of this interpretation was the introduction of the concept of
traditional occupational under-representation—a key feature of much
subsequent policy. The Women's Information Service was shortly
subsumed within the Equal Opportunities Unit established in 1976,
which subsequently became the originator of a series of Equal Opportunities Action Programmes.

The first Equal Opportunities Action Programme (1982–85) (CEC
1982c) that covered the middle section of the period of this chapter, had
little impact and was generally ignored until the Recommendation of
1984 (CEC 1984). This subsequent Recommendation on 'positive action
for women' encouraged the participation of women in various occupations where they were under-represented, especially 'in the sectors of
the future and at higher levels of responsibility in order to achieve
better use of all human resources' (CEC 1984: 34). It added that steps
should be taken to provide more vocational choice, and more relevant
vocational skills, and to encourage women into those sectors, prof-
essions and levels where they were under-represented, particularly with
regard to positions of responsibility. In line with the more widespread
concern over new technology, it stated that efforts should be made to
encourage women into their use and development. The Recommendation was clearly concerned with under-representation but, unlike the
interpretation of WIS, actually made no reference to 'traditional' but
instead emphasized, first, the 'future sectors of employment' related to
the growth and impact of new technologies, and second, the need to
address hierarchical under-representation.

The Second Action Programme that covered the years 1986–90 (CEC
1985f), however, continued to focus on *traditional* occupational under-
representation. It ignored the Recommendation's concern with hierarchical under-representation, and paid only lip-service to its emphasis
on new technologies. The Action Programme simply appended 'new
technology' to the general descriptor of occupational under-representation. Around the same time, although the fourth reform of the Fund
(considered below) continued to designate *women* as a priority group, it
defined eligibility far more closely—that is, those women who were

unemployed and with few qualifications or marketable skills. Despite the emphasis that the Equal Opportunities Unit had placed upon it, the term 'traditional' was not mentioned in this reform,[2] nor in the subsequent Guidelines (CEC 1989c) that followed the fourth reform (CEC 1988a). These Fund documents simply stressed the 'integration of women in occupations where they are substantially underrepresented' (CEC 1989c: 9).

This focus on women has highlighted just one of the social groups that was targeted, from the first reform on, by the Fund. It has also drawn attention to the relationship between the Fund and other Community policies. The exploration of this particular relationship is continued in the following chapter where the analysis is centred on the third and fourth Action Programmes (CEC 1991a; 1995b).

Combining the Structural Funds: 1988

The key Regulation combining the Structural Funds (CEC 1988e) established the foundations upon which the fourth reform of the Fund (CEC 1988a) would be based. The predicted effects of the completed single market provided the impetus for this major legislation that outlined the tasks of the combined Structural Funds. Most importantly it stated that the Structural Funds would be redistributed within a framework of five priority 'objectives':

> Objective 1: 'promoting the development and structural adjustment of those regions whose development [was] lagging behind';
> Objective 2: 'converting the regions, frontier regions or parts of regions … seriously affected by industrial decline';
> Objective 3: 'combat long-term unemployment';
> Objective 4: 'facilitate the occupational integration of young people';
> Objective 5: 'speed up the adjustment of agricultural structures';
> Objective 5b: 'promote the development of rural areas' (CEC 1988e: 11).

The Social Fund was to be involved in all objectives except 5a and, moreover, it was the only Structural Fund that would address objectives 3 and 4: long-term unemployment and the occupational integration of young people. The Structural Funds Regulation also redefined the tasks

2.   The significance of the concept of 'traditional' is, during this period, most clearly evident in the ESF programme guidelines. For an account of this see Brine (1992).

of the Social Fund and declared that first, 'the essential tasks of the ESF [were to combat] long-term unemployment and the occupational integration of young people'; second, to 'help to support economic and social cohesion; and third, it was an 'instrument of decisive importance in the promotion of consistent employment policies in the Member States and in the Community' (CEC 1988e: 9). The Structural Funds Regulation thereby highlighted three of the main themes that run throughout this analysis: the sub-discourses of social exclusion and social cohesion, and the Commission's determined efforts to make the Fund a proactive instrument of the developing European employment strategy.

The Structural Funds Regulation was built on four basic principles. First, it concentrated effort onto the regions whose development was lagging behind and areas of industrial decline, and onto long-term and young unemployed people. Second, it introduced the concept of partnership, in which the Commission and the Member States—at national, regional and local levels—were to act as partners 'within the framework of its responsibilities and powers, in the pursuit of a common goal' (CEC 1988e: 10). Furthermore, it explicitly stated that Community action was 'intended to be complementary to action by the Member States [and] to back up national measures' (p. 10). Third was the concept of programming that, related to multiannual programmes, was to lead to the Social Fund's own initiatives. Finally, the difficult and tendentious concept of additionality was somewhat clarified to mean that increased Fund allocations were to be matched by the Member State's equivalent increase in their national expenditure—that is, Community funds could not simply be used to replace Member State expenditure.[3]

Specifically with regard to the Social Fund, the Structural Funds Regulation strengthened the key discursive shift identified in the third reform (CEC 1983d) that had removed the Treaty's requirement that training should lead to employment. The 1988 Structural Funds Regulation fundamentally changed the aim of the Social Fund: the Treaty of Rome had stated that the Fund was to promote employment facilities and occupational and geographical mobility; this was now changed to combating long-term unemployment and facilitating the occupational integration of young people. The focus had changed from employment to unemployment.

3.   See also Harrop (1996) on additionality.

Fourth Reform of the ESF: The 1988 Regulation

Following the Regulation on the Structural Funds (CEC 1988e), the fourth reform presented a critical restructuring of the Fund (CEC 1988a). While it continued to be focused on specific social groups, these were nevertheless subsidiary to the new concerns of the Fund: long-term and youth unemployment, and regional 'disparity'. Even in the non-prioritized regions, priority was given to measures that would 'meet the requirements and prospects of the labour market' (CEC 1988e: 23). The fourth reform continued the trend whereby the redistributive qualities of the Social Fund were focused onto those social groups and geographic regions of perceived greatest need, with a particular emphasis on the regions classified as objective 1, and to a lesser extent, objective 2.

The divulged Member State administration of the Fund was strengthened, as were the parameters that were defined by the Commission, hence the tension between the Member States and the Commission, evident from the beginning of the Fund, continued in the run up to the completion of the single market. These Commission-defined parameters were constructed partly through the new three-year Guidelines for objectives 3 and 4, and partly through the introduction of 'on-the-spot' monitoring checks. The Guidelines, published in 1989, were concerned only with the 'unemployment' objectives 3 and 4 (CEC 1989c). Enacting the demands of the Structural Funds Regulation, each Member State was now required to present to the Commission a Plan that detailed the way in which the Fund would be integrated into their national training and labour market strategy. This would lead to national Community Support Frameworks (CSFs) agreed between individual Member States and the Commission. Henceforth, Member States were to provide a great deal of national labour market information that would include data on the disparity between job applications and vacancies (including 'female employment'), details of unfilled vacancies and labour market opportunities, and of course, the training measures that were to be implemented.

The other key features of this fourth reform were first, that it introduced vocational guidance; second, that it ring-fenced funding for particular concerns; third that it widened the definition of vocational training; and fourth, that it allowed for a much wider range of measures to take place within 'objective 1' regions.

The fourth reform addressed the need for vocational guidance that had been made in the Council Resolution of 1980 (CEC 1980). It was, at that time, simply appended to the 'vocational training operations' stated in the general scope of eligible operations, but was nevertheless important for guidance would in future become a highly significant contributor to the general discursive shift away from the originally stated aims of employment towards the redefined aim of the 'employ-ability' of the unemployed.

The other eligible operation of the Fund related once again to job creation. The process that had begun in the second reform and expanded in the third, was now enlarged further to include 'subsidies for recruitment to newly created stable jobs [and] the creation of self-employed activities' (CEC 1988a: 21). Furthermore, financial support was, for a limited period of three years, extended to provide recruitment subsidies for long-term unemployed people aged over 25 that were to be employed, for at least six months, in 'non-productive projects [that fulfilled] a public need'.

The second significant development in the fourth reform was the introduction of a ring-fenced proportion of the Fund for proactive measures that reflected the Commission's increased concern with unemployment. Five per cent was set aside to finance innovatory schemes, measures that included studies, technical assistance and the exchange of experience, and the transfer and dissemination of good practice. Social Fund 'initiatives' produced three notable Community programmes: Euroform, focused on vocational training and employ-ment opportunities; Horizon, focused on training for people with disabilities; and NOW—New Opportunities for Women (that is, women returning to the labour market after, for example, a period of caring for their children). In this way, the Commission further strengthened its own position with regard to the proactive role of the Fund. The domi-nant theme throughout this fourth reform was undoubtedly that of rising unemployment, especially in 'objective 1' regions.

Until now, the working definition of vocational training had contin-ued basically unchanged since the Treaty of Rome (CEC 1957) and its emphasis on employment and occupational and geographical mobility. However, the changing nature of the labour market and the consequent demands upon training led, in the fourth reform, to a redefinition in which vocational training was now considerably broadened to include:

any measure aimed at providing the skills necessary to carry out one or more specific types of employment, with the exception of apprenticeship schemes, and any measure with the relevant technology content required by technological change and requirements and developments on the labour market' (CEC 1988a: 22).

This redefinition thereby acknowledged the changes that were taking place in the labour market, most particularly the move towards the less secure employment of a post-Fordist economy, and thus led to a call for more generic skills, especially those linked to the new technologies. While exempting apprenticeship schemes from the general scope of vocational training, it was, as detailed below, nevertheless allowed within the priority objective 1 regions. The general trend of prioritization, apparent throughout this fourth reform, continued within the Community-wide objectives 3 and 4; their emphasis first on the 'occupational integration' of adults who had been unemployed for at least twelve months, and second, on those aged under 25, 'however long or short the period during which they have been seeking employment' (CEC 1988a: 22).

The range of measures available to 'objective 1' regions were greater than in the non-priority regions. For instance, in 'objective 1' regions the Fund would finance the theoretical non-work based portion of apprenticeship training and would also provide recruitment subsidies to long-term unemployed adults. In a rather unclear passage the fourth reform also stated that in these top priority regions, vocational training would be even further broadened to include:

in specific cases to be defined according to the particular needs of the countries and regions concerned, that part of national secondary, or corresponding education systems specifically devoted to vocational training following compulsory full-time schooling where that part meets the challenges posed by economic and technological changes (CEC 1988a: 22).

Here, the Fund, pushing at the limits of its legal competence, attempted to influence the vocational needs of the compulsory schooling sector— particularly those young people (those with fewest qualifications) who were most likely to become unemployed. Whereas the sub-discourses of social cohesion and exclusion are strengthened in this fourth reform, the major emphasis on exclusion is from within the strengthened discourse of social cohesion—that is, from within the newly created priority 1 regions.

The following year the Commission produced Guidelines for objective 3 and 4 of the Fund—those objectives concerned with long-term and youth unemployment (CEC 1989c). These objectives applied across the entire Community and applications for funding were not to be selected on the basis of regionalization but 'on qualitative factors, in particular on the requirements and prospects of the labour market' (CEC 1989c: 7). Explicit reference continued to be made to unemployment and the needs of the labour market. The Guidelines recognized that the single market would 'reveal new training needs and ... make a higher general level of qualification even more necessary' (p. 6); it described an 'evolving' world of work where 'occupational hierarchies are shifting, old occupations are disappearing or changing in content and new ones are emerging' (CEC 1989c: 6). The fourth reform and its accompanying Guidelines stressed the importance of using the Fund to create 'stable' jobs; this, ironically, in stark contrast to the picture of an unstable labour market that was otherwise presented throughout both documents. The Guidelines stated that 'the extension of the duration of unemployment is the most significant and worrying phenomenon to have affected the labour market of the Community in recent years'; nearly six million people had been unemployed for more than one year, and five million people aged under 25 were also 'seeking work' (CEC 1989c: 6). Although the previous third reform (CEC 1983a) had removed the direct link between training and employment, the fourth reform and its Guidelines continued to repeatedly stress the centrality of the labour market. Yet, despite the explicit concern with human resources, it is, at the same time, possible to discern the emergent sub-discourse of social exclusion: for instance, in training measures for the long-term unemployed, priority was given to 'the development of operations combining several types of intervention in order that training should be a real factor in promoting occupational and *social* integration' (CEC 1989c: 8).

Despite Article 130 of the SEA (CEC 1986a) and references to economic and social cohesion, the overwhelming emphasis of the fourth reform was on unemployment—within the non-priority as well as the newly established priority 1 and 2 areas. The reform attempted to make the Fund as flexible as possible in the measures that it would support, yet at the same time, it was as tightly targeted as possible onto those regions and social groups most in need. Finally, the Fund, still precariously balanced between the Commission and the Member State, had become a more significant instrument of Community policy, and concerned as it was with unemployment, it was at that time, placed in a pivotal position between the earlier dominance of the discourse of economic growth and the emergent sub-discourse of social exclusion.

Discursive Shifts

The theme of this chapter has been the changing labour market and the growing concern with the unemployed worker. The emergent discourse of the flexible worker that was identified in the previous chapter, was no longer that of changing occupation or skill, but of movement between employment and unemployment within a rapidly changing and unstable labour market. The previous chapter identified an early concern with Member State responsibility for structural changes in the economy; this too continued throughout this period as the enormity of the changes impacted on the European Community and the Member State. Further labour market changes were generated by the construction of the European single market and by the increasing impact of new technologies. Seen by many as a period of change from a Fordist to a post-Fordist economy, these were years in which the economic and social consequences of the single market dominated and, to address these fundamental structural changes, the Fund was critically refocused, first onto the young and long-term unemployed (exclusion) and second, onto the regions of greatest deprivation and unemployment (cohesion). It was the period in which, despite the repeatedly stressed importance of the labour market, the original demand that training would lead to training-related employment was removed—for it was no longer even remotely achievable.

The discursive shifts identified in this chapter reflect the economic, political and emergent social concerns that permeated this period. While the oil crisis, changing demography and new technology were affecting the labour market and unemployment was already rising, this was a period of foreboding and warning; the Community prepared itself for further changes in employment patterns brought about by the completion of the single market and further new technological developments.

It could be argued that the most visible discourse, related to the dominant discourse of economic growth, was the sub-discourse of human resources. References to employability were voiced throughout the period and, moreover, were linked to the first words of a sub-discourse of pathologization (CEC 1980). Yet, beneath this clear concern with the flexible worker and their 'employability', there was a clear sub-text that expressed the fear of rising unemployment and the consequent threat to economic, social and political stability—the strengthened sub-discourse of social exclusion. A similar fear of instability centred on the possibility of increased regional disparities brought about in part by the completion of the single market—a similar strengthening of the sub-discourse of social cohesion. These threats to stability, while linked in part to the dominant discourse of economic growth, were more immediately linked to the dominant discourse of political stability and the construction of the Community. Hence, drifting out from these dominant economic and political discourses was not only the sub-discourse of human resources but also the emerging sub-discourses of social cohesion, social exclusion and pathologization. The sub-discourse of social cohesion related primarily to the single market and regional disparities; the sub-discourse of social exclusion to the disadvantages of particular social groups; that of pathologization to the perceived lack of social as well as vocational skills by unemployed young people. The interplay between these two concerns would continue throughout the rest of the twentieth century and into the twenty-first, for they are directly related to the more fundamental shifts that take place within the dominant economic and political discourses of the Community/Union.

4 |

The ESF and Social Exclusion: 1989–1996

Political, Economic and Policy Context

The years immediately following the fourth Social Fund reform of 1988 were ones of immense upheaval that swept through the political map of Europe: in 1989 the Berlin Wall was breached; a year later Germany was reunified which led, George (1996) argues, to renewed concerns among the other members of the Community. The first concern was that Germany would begin to focus its attention on Central and Eastern Europe rather than on the Community; the second was that 'the reunified German state would rediscover its nationalist inclinations and start to dominate its partners' (George 1996: 16). Other events of this time included, in 1990, the start of the Gulf War, the disintegration of Yugoslavia and the release from prison of Nelson Mandela. This was followed, in 1991, by the break-up of the Soviet Union, and in 1994 by Mandela's election as President of South Africa. The reunification of Germany and the collapse of Communism provided the impetus for the Community's move towards political as well as monetary union. These years were therefore significant ones for the process of widening and deepening the Community: the Intergovernmental Conference (IGC) that began in December 1990, concluded in 1991 at Maastricht with the Treaty of the European Union (CEC 1992a); the single market itself was completed in 1992.

The relationship between the Commission and the Member States was extremely tense during these years, epitomized first in the relationship between the Commission President Jacques Delors and the UK Prime Minister Margaret Thatcher, and secondly in the political processes surrounding the Maastricht IGC and the ratification of the Treaty. It has been argued that the Treaty itself reflected a compromise between supranationalism and intergovernmentalism: 'it faces both ways: towards intergovernmentalism and towards some kind of "federal vocation"' (McAllister 1997: 225). Post-Maastricht, the new principle of subsidiarity limited Community action to those policy areas that could clearly be handled better at Community level than national. At the same time the powers of the European Parliament were increased, thereby giving them greater involvement in the policy-making process. Finally, towards the end of this period, the Community—or as it became known post-Maastricht, the Union (EU)—was, in 1995, further enlarged to include the new Member States of Austria, Finland and Sweden, thereby extending its northern edge. These years, dominated by the Delors presidency, end with the incoming president, Jacques Santer.

Economically, the impact of technological change on production, of economic globalization, and of demographic change continued; added to these were the newer economic consequences of German reunification, Communist collapse and Community expansion. The major trends of the previous period continued: traditional heavy industry remained in decline while service industries continued to rise. While new technologies continued to have a major impact, their opportunities were at last becoming apparent, particularly in the information, communication and bio-medical fields. Generally, the period remained one of considerable change as unemployment continued to rise and the labour market shifted from a Fordist to a post-Fordist model of production that brought an emphasis on flexibility, core skills and lack of job security.

The policies that affected the Social Fund were predominantly those related to the construction of the European Union itself: the single market and the Treaty. As detailed in the previous chapter, the Single European Act (SEA) had already impacted on the fourth reform of the Fund. The SEA continued to affect policy, particularly through the inclusion of the Fund within the Structural Funds, and the emphasis on economic and social cohesion that had been introduced through SEA Article 130 (CEC 1986b). Anderson summarized the significance of these changes in the following way:

> The ESF's social policy affinities ... could enable the Social Fund to function as a bridge between the Structural Funds and social policies directed at entitled individuals ... The Social Fund becomes linked ... to the much broader problem of poverty, which has increasingly become a manifestation of unemployment. This opens up the possibility that two quite different policy models, those that address human capital development and others that address the problems of poverty, can be joined (Anderson 1995: 154-55).

Apart from the Regulation that amended the Structural Funds (CEC 1993c), other notable policies of the period included the Charter of

Social Rights (CEC 1989a) and the two major White Papers: *Growth, Competitiveness, Employment* (CEC 1993b), and *European Social Policy* (CEC 1994a) with its explicit definition of social exclusion (Littlewood *et al.* 1999; Atkinson and Davoudi 2000). It was also the period in which, among many innovative policies, the White Paper on education and training was produced (CEC 1995a) and equal opportunities were mainstreamed throughout all Structural Funds (CEC 1996a). Most significantly for the Fund, this was the period which saw the extension of European social policy and by implication a readjustment of the Fund itself. However, among this unprecedented interest in social policy, there was only one major piece of ESF policy during this period; this was the 1993 Regulation that detailed the fifth reform (CEC 1993a). Nevertheless, as this brief overview has illustrated, these years from 1989 to 1996 were ones of major political, economic and hence, policy changes.

The early 1990s were the years in which the previously predicted rise in unemployment materialized: 16 million in 1992 (CEC 1992b); 17 million in 1993 (CEC 1993b), and a forecast 18 million in 1995 (CEC 1994a).[1] The trends identified in the previous chapter continued: the decline of heavy manufacturing industry; the rise of service industries and new information and communication industries. As previously predicted, these new technological advances had an enormous impact on almost all aspects of the labour market and on the economy more generally. Most significantly, the single market came to fruition at the end of 1992.

The chapter begins by considering the Treaty of the European Union (CEC 1992a), most specifically Article 3 relating to the Social Fund. It then considers the relationship between the Fund and the development of broader social policy. The next section focuses on the major reforms of this period—first, the Regulation that amended the Structural Funds (CEC 1993c), and second, the fifth reform Regulation (CEC 1993a). The following section returns again to the analysis of the relationship between the Fund and the discourse of equal opportunities that began in the previous chapter. The next section considers the relationship between the Fund and the broader vocational training discourse that was developing at that time, especially that relating to youth and

---

1.   Despite the efforts to combat unemployment, the Council stated, in 2000, that there were still more than 15 million Europeans out of work—a decrease of only 1 million since 1992 (CEC 2000a).

unemployment. This is followed by the main section of the chapter, which focuses on the White Papers related to unemployment and social exclusion. The final section considers the discursive shifts that took place between 1989 and 1996.

The ESF and the Treaty of the European Union

The Treaty that established the European Union (CEC 1992a) defined its first objective:

> to promote economic and social progress which is balanced and sustainable, in particular through the creation of an area without internal frontiers, through the strengthening of economic and social cohesion and through the establishment of economic and monetary union, ultimately including a single currency in accordance with the provisions of this Treaty (CEC 1992a: 7).

Article 3 stated that there would be 'a policy in the social sphere comprising a European Social Fund' which would contribute to 'education and training of quality' (p. 12). Note here, for the first time, the inclusion of education as well as training. Furthermore, blurring the boundaries between the sub-discourse of human resources and the sub-discourse of social exclusion, the Treaty's *Agreement on Social Policy* stressed the importance of the development of human resources, not only with a view to lasting high employment, but also with the aim of combating exclusion.

The new Title VIII, on social policy, education, vocational training and youth, introduced new areas of concern to the Fund. It made slight but nevertheless notable amendments to the original 1957 key Article 123 (CEC 1957) previously discussed in Chapter 2. It stated that:

> In order to improve employment opportunities for workers in the internal market and to contribute thereby to raising the standard of living, a European Social Fund is hereby established in accordance with the provisions set out below; *it shall aim to render the employment of workers easier* and to increase their geographical and occupational mobility within the Community, and to *facilitate their adaptation to industrial changes and to changes in production systems, in particular through vocational training and retraining* (CEC 1992a: 46; emphasis added to illustrate the amendments to the original treaty).

While there were no actual omissions from the existing Article 123, the significant additions shown in italics illustrate the proactive measures that the Fund was to take. Greater effort was needed; first, to pre-empt unemployment caused by industrial and technological change, and second, to actively promote 'new' employment. Other notable changes to the general educational and vocational field that surrounded the Fund were found in Articles 126 and 127. Article 126 created a new legal competency related to 'the development of quality education by encouraging cooperation between Member States ... [and by] developing the European dimension in education' (p. 47). Article 127 replaced the original Article 128 (see Appendix 3) and made a significant shift away from the earlier emphasis on 'common policy' and 'harmonious development' for, in the spirit of subsidiarity, it now 'fully respected' the 'responsibility of the Member States for the content and organization of vocational training', and moreover would exclude 'any harmonization of the laws and regulations of the Member States' (CEC 1992a: 48). As in the new Article 123, Article 127 similarly referred to the need to 'facilitate adaptation to industrial changes' and 'to facilitate vocational integration and reintegration into the labour market'.

A further consequential feature of the Treaty of the Union was that which, building on the SEA (CEC 1986b), was covered by Article 130—economic and social cohesion: namely, the reduction of 'disparities between the levels of development of the various regions and the backwardness of the least favoured regions'—a reduction which it would achieve through the use of the Structural Funds (CEC 1992a: 53). Cohesion thus became one of the three pillars of the EU, along with economic and monetary union and the single market. Cohesion was further emphasized in the accompanying *Protocol on Economic and Social Cohesion* which reaffirmed the conviction that the Structural Funds were to 'play a considerable part in the achievement of Community objectives in the field of cohesion' (CEC 1992a: 203). Article 130 both consolidated the regional prioritization introduced a few years previously by the fourth reform (CEC 1988a) and by the Regulation related to the Structural Funds (CEC 1988e), that were considered in the previous chapter. Article 130 pointed forwards to the greater emphasis on social cohesion that is the central feature of the following chapter.

The ESF and Social Policy

In 1989 the Council adopted the Decision (CEC 1989d) that established an action programme concerning the economic and social integration of the 'economically and socially less privileged groups in society' (p. 10); note the recognition of social as well as economic lack of privilege, and the need for social as well as economic integration. The action programme built on the previous Decision to combat poverty (CEC 1985b), and referred to the growth of the 'phenomenon of insecurity' in employment. It also reaffirmed its intention to 'attack the structural causes of this economic and social exclusion, [and thereby] to make an effective contribution to the fight against it'. Apart from its contribution to the general construction of the sub-discourse of social exclusion, this Decision also had relevance for the Social Fund, for it stressed the importance of 'overall coherence' between all Community operations that had an impact on the 'economically and socially less privileged groups in society' (CEC 1989d: 11). With the exception of the demand for 'policy coherence', however, there was, despite the recognition of the structural causes of unemployment, little to offer in the way of strategies with which to mount such an attack.

In the same year the *Community Charter of the Fundamental Social Rights of Workers* (CEC 1989a) was published. There were three important developments within this Charter: first, it pushed forward the social dimension of the single market, and paved the way for the social agreement within the Treaty of the European Union; second, it developed and extended the sub-discourse of social exclusion to include broader issues of discrimination; and third, it reaffirmed the rights of adults and young people to vocational training. All three themes were subsequently taken up and further developed within the Fund.

While the Charter was directly linked to the completion of the single market and the dominant discourse of economic growth, it also introduced a social dimension into the single market. Although it referred solely to workers, it nevertheless 'solemnly declared' that 'the implementation of the Single European Act must take full account of the social dimension of the Community' (p. 4). First in its list of objectives was the need to promote employment and combat unemployment. Significant in the pre-Maastricht construction of the sub-discourse of social exclusion was the fact that exclusion was no longer linked only to unemployment but to other forms of discrimination also, including 'discrimination on the grounds of race, colour and religion' (CEC 1989a: 3).

'Vocational training throughout working life' was, within the Charter, given the status of a 'Right', as was that of school-leavers to receive two years of 'initial vocational training in order to adapt to the requirements of their future working life' (p. 18). The significance of this was evident within the subsequent development of vocational training policy for young unemployed people as illustrated in the discussion below.

Reform of the Structural Funds: 1993

The Structural Funds Regulation (CEC 1993c) established the foundations upon which the subsequent fifth reform of the Fund (CEC 1993a) was based, for it maintained, strengthened and reinforced the four major innovatory principles of the Regulation that had first combined the Structural Funds (CEC 1988e): concentration of effort, partnership, programming and additionality. The Structural Funds were to be more effective, simpler and more transparent with details provided on the allocations made for each objective to each Member State.

The new Regulation amended the objectives of the first Structural Funds Regulation (CEC 1988e) detailed in Chapter 3. Objective 1 remained focused on regions 'whose development lagged behind'. Following the reunification of Germany, objective 1 included the five new German *Länder* and East Berlin.[2] As part of the new emphasis on regional economic and social cohesion, objective 1 was more tightly targeted on to regions rather than an entire Member State. Objective 2 remained focused on those regions (including urban communities) that were 'seriously affected by industrial decline'. Eligibility was based primarily on unemployment figures, with further emphasis on unemployment caused by industrial change and by changes in production. Particular attention was directed towards areas, especially urban areas, with severe problems linked to derelict industrial sites. Again as a result of German reunification, West Berlin was specifically mentioned as an area that would qualify for objective 2 status. Objective 3 was now widened to include both adult and young unemployed people. The new objective 4 was focused on those workers vulnerable to industrial change and to changes in production systems. The new objective 5b was introduced, in anticipation of the new Scandinavian members, with the intention of developing sparsely populated areas.

2.   Within the UK, Northern Ireland, northern Scotland and Merseyside were given objective 1 status.

Approximately one-third of the total EU budget was allocated to the Structural Funds (that is, 138 billion ecu), of which 30% (42 billion ecu) was directed to the Social Fund. With specific regard to the Social Fund, the Structural Funds Regulation stated that its priority task was to combat unemployment. There were four approaches to this task: to facilitate access to the labour market; to promote equal opportunities in the labour market; to develop skills, abilities and professional qualifications; and to encourage job creation.

More generally, the Structural Funds Regulation stressed the importance of complementarity, partnership and evaluation. With regard to complementarity, the Regulation declared that 'Community operations shall be such as to complement or contribute to corresponding national operations' (CEC 1993c: 8). In relation to partnership, it stated that the Commission, the Member States and other authorities, bodies or parties at national, regional or local level, would act together in pursuit of a common goal. Evaluation and monitoring were further emphasized, especially in relation to the concern with economic and social cohesion introduced through Article 130 of the Single European Act (CEC 1986b) and consolidated in the TEU (CEC 1992a). Finally, the Regulation reinforced the Commission's demand for national plans, Community Support Frameworks and indicative financing plans.

Fifth Reform of the ESF: The 1993 Regulation

Following the Regulation on the Structural Funds (CEC 1993c) the fifth reform of the Social Fund (CEC 1993a) reinforced the emphasis on the consolidation of effort. It stressed, first, that the Fund should be targeted onto those social groups and regions of greatest need; second, that objectives 3 and 4 were amended; third, that the concept of vocational training was extended; fourth, that vocational guidance was given greater priority, and furthermore, was linked to the newly introduced concept of counselling; and fifth, the Fund was henceforth to operate within the principle of subsidiarity.

The dominant features throughout all the objectives were that the Fund should be targeted onto those social groups and regions in greatest need, and that its scope be expanded so that, from within its targeted position, it would be as flexible as possible in relation to the measures that it would support. For instance, it now allowed for the training of those professionals who would work with unemployed people. It also firmed up, within the general scope of operations, the option of vocational guidance that had been introduced in the fourth reform (CEC 1988a). The fifth reform gave vocational guidance far greater priority, including it, along with vocational training, within its top priority actions for addressing long-term unemployment. Moreover, specifically within objective 3 and 4, vocational guidance was linked to the newly introduced concept of 'counselling'. The priority measure for long-term unemployment also introduced the concept of pre-training and the upgrading of basic skills. These measures, related explicitly to the sub-discourse of human resources, simultaneously strengthened the sub-discourse of pathologization. Finally, a new measure of 'temporary employment aids' was also introduced—aids for geographical mobility, recruitment and the creation of self-employed activities.

In line with the Regulation on the Structural Funds (CEC 1993c), the Social Fund read:

> objective 3: 'to [combat] long term unemployment and to [facilitate] the integration into working life of young people and of persons exposed to exclusion from the labour market' (CEC 1993a: 39).

The rationale for this change was the 'seriousness of the unemployment situation' (p. 39); objective 3 would combat long-term unemployment and facilitate the integration of young people into working life. The last priority would be given towards all other persons exposed to exclusion from the labour market—such as women returners. Meanwhile, the new objective 4 read:

> objective 4: 'to facilitate the adaptation of workers of either sex, especially those threatened with unemployment, to industrial change and to changes in production systems' (CEC 1993a: 40).

This was a notable change because it extended the Fund to include those people who were still in employment, albeit in employment of a vulnerable nature. Once again, the scope of actions covered by the Fund was broad, for the new objective 4 strengthened employment and job qualifications 'through anticipation, counselling, networking and train-ing operations'; it was aimed at workers threatened with unemploy-ment. For the first time, moving further towards proactive preventative measures, the Regulation stressed that operations under objective 4 were to 'address the underlying causes of problems relating to industrial adaptation ... and not deal with symptoms relating to the short-term market' (p. 39). Once again, measures included vocational training, retraining, guidance and counselling.[3]

The previous chapter detailed the way in which the fourth reform had, for objective 1 regions only, extended the definition of vocational training to include provision during the latter years of compulsory schooling. As a consequence of the 'serious and deteriorating situation concerning unemployment' described in the Resolution on employment (CEC 1992b), the fifth reform extended this definition to the non-priority of regions covered by objective 3. It referred to:

> the possibility of vocational training equivalent to compulsory school-
> ing, provided that by the end of that training the young people are old
> enough to join the labour market (CEC 1993a: 40).

The fifth reform continued to include, for unemployed school-leavers, two years (or more) initial vocational training that would lead to a vocational qualification. There were two highly significant features to this focus on young people: first, the extension back to pre-school leavers not only pointed to the seriousness of youth unemployment but also enabled the Commission to gain a further toehold in the field of compulsory schooling; second, the Fund, in furthering the discourse of pathologization, did not explicitly refer to their unemployed status as such, but to their 'search of employment' and their 'occupational inte-gration'; thus it constructed a labour market which was waiting to welcome them, rather than one which, in reality, was extremely difficult to break into.

As part of the overall process of subsidiarity confirmed in the Maastricht Treaty (CEC 1992a), the Reform continued to devolve decision-making and managerial power away from the Commission and onto the Member States, yet at the same time it continued to stress the dominating central intentions of the Regulation itself; for instance:

> The Member States and the Commission shall ensure that operations
> under the different objectives form a coherent approach to improving the
> workings of the labour market and developing human resources, taking
> into account the development, reconversion and structural adjustment
> objectives in the Member States or regions concerned (CEC 1993a: 41).

3.   The new objective 4 provoked a further example of the tension that surrounded the extent to which the Fund could operate as a proactive instrument of Commission policy. In the UK, the new objective 4 was firmly dismissed by the Conservative government led by Margaret Thatcher. The Labour government of 1997 quickly reversed this decision.

At the same time as the system of objectives influenced the activities of the Member States, the Commission also extended its own proactive approaches through the ring-fenced allocations introduced as the 'initiatives' of the fourth reform. The programmes of NOW, Horizon, Youthstart, Integra and Adapt were, in the fifth reform, consolidated under the new employment programme.

While the fifth reform continued to reflect both the dominant discourse of economic growth and the political sub-discourse of social cohesion, the emergent sub-discourses of exclusion and pathologization were clearly noticeable. In accordance with the Treaty's revised Article 123, the scope of the Fund was broadened to include at one end, vocational training within compulsory education, and at the other end those workers vulnerable to unemployment. The fifth reform was a response to the increased threat of unemployment and hence was tightly focused on those most in need—the long-term unemployed aged over 25, the young unemployed aged under 25, those at school who were vulnerable to unemployment, and those in paid work who were vulnerable to unemployment through industrial change. It was indeed less concerned with the social cohesion of regions than the fourth reform but more concerned with what, in the next couple of years, became known as social exclusion (but which, in 1993, was still referred to as 'exclusion from the labour market' (CEC 1993a: 39). At the same time, alongside the discursive thread of human resources woven through the Reform, the sub-discourse of pathologization, that began with the Resolution of 1980 (CEC 1980) was strengthened as unemployment was seen to result from the social and vocational inadequacies of young people rather than from the structural failures of the European labour market.

The ESF and Equal Opportunities

As in the previous period, the discourse of equal opportunities continued to have an impact on the Social Fund throughout the early 1990s and, moreover, to have an increased effect. The Council Resolution on the Third Equal Opportunities Action Programme (CEC 1991a) referred to the demand made in the Charter of Social Rights (CEC 1989a) that equal opportunities for men and women were to be assured and that actions were to be intensified in order to ensure their implementation. The Third Action Programme that covered the years 1991 to

1995 (CEC 1991a), required that equal opportunities were to be 'main-streamed' across all Commission policies and programmes. Most significant for vocational training within the Third Action Programme was the absence of any explicit reference to new or information technology, despite its considerable emphasis within the previous programme.

Two years after the start of the Third Action Programme, the fifth reform of the Fund (CEC 1993a) took the concerns of gender equality slightly more seriously. The reform demanded that Member States provide the Commission with a gendered breakdown of the statistics related to their use of the Fund and, written for the first time in non-gender specific language, it referred to both women and men and stated that the Fund would support measures that promoted 'equal opportunities for *men and* women on the labour market'. However, despite such a general preamble, it went on to prioritize measures:

> especially in areas of work in which *women* are under-represented and particularly for *women* not possessing vocational qualifications or returning to the labour market after a period of absence (CEC 1993a: 40, emphasis added).

This was an important statement because, despite the preamble reference to women and *men*, it was nevertheless clearly directed towards women. Furthermore, the reform specified those particular women that were to be targeted—that is, those women 'not possessing vocational qualifications, or returning to the labour market after a period of absence'. The Fund was therefore targeted not only at women returners but more specifically at a *particular* group of women: low- and under-educated women—those women most at risk of unemployment and social exclusion.

More significant for the development of equal opportunities policies than the fifth reform was the preceding Regulation on the Structural Funds (CEC 1993c), for it demanded that the Member States include in the labour market section of their national plan, details on the current employment position of women and the contribution that the Social Fund would make towards improving it. Furthermore, it also legitimated the Equal Opportunities Unit's demand that gendered equal opportunities be 'mainstreamed' and thereby made an enforceable principle.[4] One year later, the demand for mainstreaming was reinforced by a

---

4.   See Brine (2000) and Rees (1998) for a fuller exploration of the significance of the concept of mainstreaming.

further Council Resolution (CEC 1994b) that called on both the Member States and the Commission to ensure its implementation throughout all the Structural Funds, and most particularly within the Social Fund. A subsequent Decision, related to the Fourth Action Programme (CEC 1995c), consolidated the concept of mainstreaming, requiring its integration into *all* Community policies and programmes. The following year, this was followed by the Council's adoption of a Resolution related specifically to 'mainstreaming equal opportunities in the labour market' (CEC 1996a).

In promoting 'competitiveness and economic growth', mainstreaming equality was directly related to the dominant discourse of economic growth and represented the most significant shift in the discourse of equal opportunities during the early 1990s. As this coincided with the Fund's focused attention on the long-term unemployed, the young unemployed and those vulnerable to unemployment, it meant that women were to be automatically included in any measures provided through these broader concerns.[5] At this time 'women' were the third most important social group within the Fund, following the long-term unemployed and the young unemployed. A central aim of 'mainstreaming' within the Fund was the recognition of long-term unemployed women and young unemployed women as well as women returners and those wishing to enter non-traditional occupations.

Vocational Training and the Young Unemployed

Throughout the late 1980s and early 1990s there was a growing concern over the numbers of unemployed young people, for instance in 1993 over 20% of young people were unemployed (CEC 1993b) and, inevitably, both the fourth and fifth reforms of the Fund targeted resources more and more tightly at youth unemployment. Moreover, this concern was further developed through non-ESF training programmes such as Petra (CEC 1987b; 1991b), Leonardo da Vinci (CEC 1994c), and the White Paper on education and training (CEC 1995a). It was also the period in which the Youth for Europe (YfE) programme was developed (CEC 1991c; 1995d); however, YfE was concerned not with vocational training but with promoting cultural and racial tolerance.

---

5. As shown in Brine (2000), within the UK, the immediate effect of mainstreaming was the marginalization of provision for women.

The initial competency for Petra was Article 128 of the Treaty of the EEC and not that related to the Fund—Article 123. The first Petra programme covered the years 1988–92, and four years later, a further Decision on Petra (CEC 1991b) reiterated the statement that originated in the Charter of Social Rights, that young people be 'entitled' to initial vocational training to enable them to adapt to the requirements of their future working life (CEC 1989a). Unlike the Social Fund, Petra extended the definition of 'young people' to include those aged up to 28; it also extended the scope of financial support to include periods of training or work experience in other Member States; and finally, it stressed the importance of 'complementarity' between Petra and the Social Fund. Whereas Petra, like the Fund, was more concerned with the preparation of young people for *working* life, the emphasis in Youth for Europe was turned towards the broader concept of 'adult' life, fostered especially through youth exchanges and mobility throughout the Community.

The Leonardo da Vinci Programme (CEC 1994c), and the White Paper on education and training (CEC 1995a), again focused attention on the training needs of unemployed people and, most particularly, those of young people. The Decision that established Leonardo (an action programme for a Community vocational training policy), in line with the general policy sentiments following the TEU, expressed the importance of subsidiarity, consistency and complementarity between itself and the Structural Funds. From within the overall dominant discourse of economic growth, Leonardo was framed not only by the sub-discourse of human resources but also by the then rapidly emerging sub-discourse of social exclusion discussed below. It stressed the training needs of young people and reiterated the commitment to provide vocational training for school-leavers. Moreover, it singled out 'disadvantaged young people without adequate training and in particular young people who [left] the education system without adequate training' (CEC 1994c: 12).

The focus on 'disadvantaged' and 'low-educated' youth continued as a major concern within the White Paper on education and training (CEC 1995a). The White Paper referred to the concept of social exclusion that had been developed within the White Paper on social policy discussed below (CEC 1994a). The Education and Training White Paper developed the main themes of unemployment, social exclusion and the free movement of people, and with specific regard to young people, advocated both 'second chance schools' and a European 'voluntary service'. Taking a broader focus than that permitted within the Social Fund, the White Paper pointed to the growing numbers of school exclusions and to the broad social, economic and familial context of 'disadvantage'; moreover, it declared that 'without qualifi-cations, [young people had] little hope of finding a job and thus of integrating into society' (CEC 1995a: 40).

The focus on youth unemployment during these years highlighted both the close relationship and the shifting tensions that were present between the dominant economic and political discourses and the emergent sub-discourse of social exclusion. This was pursued not only through programmes such as Petra and Leonardo but also through the key White Papers of the period that are discussed below. Nevertheless, policies such as those of Petra, Youth for Europe and Leonardo, enabled by the looser Articles 128 (EEC Treaty) and 126 (TEU) were able quickly and more explicitly to extend the scope of action beyond the labour market.[6] Yet, at the same time, the need for vocational quali-fications was constantly reiterated, as was the need for complementarity with the Social Fund.

The Fund itself, through its fifth reform of 1993 had given equal prominence to the training needs of 'the long-term unemployed' and of young people, whom it was necessary to 'integrate' into the labour market. The inference from this is that the problem of the young was one of integration rather than employment, hence the need not only for vocational training but also for guidance, counselling and basic skills. The sub-discourse constructed around young unemployed people at this time was one not so much framed by economic growth and human resources as by the emergent sub-discourse of social exclusion. Further glimmerings of what would become a sub-discourse of pathologization are identifiable in this period: a discourse that constructed the unem-ployed individual as lacking both vocational and basic skills, and hence was increasingly in need of guidance and counselling. This pathologi-zation was further developed in the concerns with unemployment and social exclusion discussed below.

6.   The changing Article numbers are summarized in Appendix 3.

Unemployment and Social Exclusion

Throughout the publications of this period, repeated reference was made to the deepening crisis of unemployment. The employment Resolution (CEC 1992b) declared that the 'Community was faced with a very serious and deteriorating situation with regard to unemployment', a situation that threatened to become the 'central problem in the 1990s' (CEC 1992b: 3). To support this statement the Resolution provided a list of harrowing statistics: there were, at that time, 16 million unemployed people in the Community (this represented 10% of the Community's workforce); this was 400% higher than in the 1960s; 'nearly half the total number of unemployed people [had] been out of work for more than a year, and some 30% of long-term unemployed people [had] never worked at all' (p. 3). Reflecting the political sub-discourses of both social cohesion and social exclusion, the Resolution stressed that unemployment was a 'particularly serious matter for certain regions and areas of the Community, notably the less-favoured regions, and for vulnerable groups in society' (p. 4). It called upon the Commission, in its review of the Social Fund, to take particular account of its comments on training and 'other services' for the unemployed. Interestingly, these 'services' that included information, job advice, counselling and work experience, were actually prioritized above that of training and vocational education. Training priority was given to young people, but their perceived lack of basic education, training and motivation was blamed for their perceived inability to participate in the labour market. Identifiable alongside the deepening crisis of unemployment was the strengthened sub-discourse of the pathologization of the unemployed.

The key document throughout this period was the White Paper entitled *Growth, Competitiveness, Employment* (CEC 1993b). This Paper was the first of several significant documents produced by the Commission that are included here because they had a direct effect on the future development of the Fund and made a critical contribution to the sub-discourse of social exclusion.

The White Paper began by declaring that its 'one and only reason' for existence was unemployment, and stated that unemployment had actually risen to 17 million and was predicted to rise within the next year to 18 million—'a figure equal to the total populations of Belgium, Denmark and Ireland' (CEC 1993b: 40). Moreover, the unemployment rates of young people were double those of adults, with particular problems in particular regions (p. 126). The Paper identified three types of unemployment: cyclical, structural and technological, and it pointed to the particular effect of unemployment upon 'low-skilled' people; the depth of the crisis was seen as largely due to insufficient adaptation to the 'changing technological, social and international environment' (p. 49). Its main strategy for tackling unemployment was the creation of 15 million new jobs, many of which would be related to the new technologies—information, communication, bio- and eco-technological. Highlighting the enormity of technological change the Paper likened these changes to those of the first industrial revolution (CEC 1993b: 13).

Despite the enormity of the unemployment statistics the White Paper's emphasis on 'solidarity' was discursive rather than practical. It stressed, through the concept of job creation, solidarity between those who had jobs and those who did not; solidarity between generations, between the more prosperous regions and the poor or struggling regions, and 'lastly and most importantly' solidarity in the fight against social exclusion. Here it pointed to the 40 million people across the Community that lived below the poverty line and called upon each citizen to practise what it called 'neighbourly solidarity' (pp. 15-16). It went on to state that the actions to combat social exclusion were 'familiar' ones:

> renovation of stricken urban areas, construction of subsidized housing, adaptation of education systems with extra resources for children from disadvantaged backgrounds, and an active employment policy which attaches high priority to the search for an activity or training accessible to everyone rather than the registration of and payment to the unemployed, even though, in the last resort, this is still essential where all other means of social reinsertion seem, for the moment, to be exhausted (CEC 1993b: 16).

Moreover, the economic and social costs of such high unemployment were 'enormous'—an 'increased burden on social services; rising poverty, crime and ill-health; and ... increasing levels of educational underachievement' (p. 127).

Although the White Paper declared that training was the catalyst of a changing society, it rightly added that it could not be seen as the sole solution but as one part of a combination of measures within which training, as an instrument of active labour market policy, was to play 'a major role in combating unemployment, making it easier for young people to enter the labour market and promote the re-employment of the long-term unemployed' (p. 117). Specifically with regard to education, the White Paper produced yet more statistics: the proportion of people leaving school with a secondary qualification was 42%, compared with 75% in the USA and 90% in Japan; the proportion of young people in higher education was 30%, compared with 70% in the USA and 50% in Japan. It declared that:

> the problem of the failure of education ... is a particularly important and increasingly widespread factor of marginalization and economic and social exclusion (CEC 1993b: 118).

From this understanding the Paper stated that basic skills were essential for integration into society and working life.

Whereas the discourse of economic growth was dominant throughout the White Paper, the sub-discourse of social exclusion was evident throughout:

> Member States have to ensure that additional jobs are most effectively made available to those in a *disadvantaged position in the labour market* ... [T]he Community now faces the danger *of not only a dual labour market but also a dual society* (CEC 1993b: 134).

It went on to specify the particular needs of long-term unemployed adults and unemployed young people, and also stressed the need to strengthen equal opportunities policies. Significantly for the future development of the Social Fund it highlighted the importance of ESF objective 3 for measures directed towards the young unemployed, and stated that 'special efforts should be targeted at those young people leaving school with no diploma or basic qualifications'. It too, like the earlier Resolution (CEC 1992b) stressed the importance of employment services, especially those related to guidance. Unlike the Fund, the White Paper referred to 'unemployed' young people rather than the more euphemistic 'integration into working life'.

The White Paper on growth was followed one year later by the Essen Council where the first plan of action for tacking unemployment was endorsed. This was also the year in which the White Paper on social policy (CEC 1994a) was published. This again drew both on the ideas introduced in the Fundamental Social Rights of Workers (CEC 1989a) and on the conference for combating social exclusion that had been held in Copenhagen in 1993. The *Social Policy* Paper continued the emphasis on employment and training begun in the *Growth, Competitiveness, Employment* Paper (CEC 1993b), yet added that social policy went beyond employment, for it affected people 'when at work and when not at work'. Most importantly it expressed the

> conviction that economic and social progress must go hand in hand ...
> [T]he pursuit of high social standards should not be seen only as a cost
> but also as a key element in the competitive formula. It is for these
> essential reasons that the Union's social policy cannot play second string
> to economic development or the functioning of the internal market (CEC
> 1994a: 9-10).

The *Social Policy* Paper frequently reiterated the *Growth* Paper's concern with rising unemployment and with the need to create new jobs. However, it also made equally frequent reference to social exclusion, as for example in its reference to the 'unacceptably high levels of unemployment, poverty and social exclusion' (p. 10), and its recognition that 'the provision of new jobs alone—even in substantial numbers—will not lead to the elimination of social exclusion' (p. 49).

Like the *Growth* Paper, *Social Policy* similarly turned to statistics to emphasize the crisis of unemployment: the rate of unemployment was 11%, youth unemployment was more than 20%, 40% of the unemployed had been unemployed long term. It predicted that unemployment would, within the next year, stabilize at 11.6%—that is, 18 million unemployed people. Moreover, 52 million people were already living below the poverty line. Not surprisingly, unemployment was 'seen as the gravest social problem throughout the Union' (CEC 1994a: 17). However, unemployment, while part of the broader sub-discourse of social exclusion, was not the only factor, for the paper pointed to the dynamic and multidimensional processes that included, along with unemployment and/or low incomes, 'housing conditions, levels of education and opportunities, health, discrimination, citizenship and integration in the local community' (p. 49). Consequently, the Paper constructed a strong and persistent sub-discourse of social exclusion. For example, it stated that:

> The marginalization of major social groups is a challenge to the social
> cohesion of the Union ... It is clear that contemporary economic and
> social conditions tend to exclude some groups from the cycle of
> opportunities ... Social exclusion is an endemic phenomenon, stemming
> from the structural changes affecting our economies and societies. It
> threatens the social cohesion of each Member State and of the Union as a

whole ... Preventing and combating social exclusion calls for an overall mobilization of efforts and combination of both economic and social measures (CEC 1994a: 49).

With specific regard to education and training, the *Social Policy* White Paper declared that 'investment in education and training is now recognized as one of the essential requirements for the competitiveness of the Union as well as for the cohesion of our societies' (CEC 1994a: 23). It singled out for special attention those young people who left school with few basic skills and inadequate literacy, and warned that 'these unqualified school-leavers inevitably [would] become the hard-core of the long-term unemployed' (p. 23); hence, high priority was to be given to the training of the 'least-qualified' unemployed. The Paper referred to the fifth reform of the Fund (CEC 1993a) and expressed its appreciation for the more flexible approach; it also emphasized the Fund's role in making 'a carefully targeted contribution to the development of a skilled, adaptable and mobile workforce'; it then summarized the tasks of the Fund by stating that:

> the Social Fund is focused on combating long-term unemployment and exclusion from the labour market, on seeking to ensure that all our young people are given the necessary skills and the opportunity to work, on promoting equal opportunities and, in the context of the new and innovative objective 4, on helping to adapt the workforce to industrial change (CEC 1994a: 26).

The White Paper then specified three priority themes for the Fund:

- improving access to and quality of initial training and education, especially through the implementation of Youth Start;
- increasing competitiveness and preventing unemployment by adapting the workforce to the challenge of change through a systematic approach to continuing training;
- improving the employment opportunities of those exposed to long-term unemployment and exclusion, through the development of a package of measures which form a pathway of reintegration (CEC 1994a: 27).

In a cursory nod to the demands of mainstreaming equal opportunities, it added that 'promoting equal opportunities for women in the labour market is an integral part to all these themes' (p. 27).

While within the *Social Policy* White Paper the discourse of economic growth itself remained strong, the sub-discourse of social exclusion was defined, made explicit and hence, considerably strengthened. The problem was no longer seen as simply that of unemployment, of exclusion from the labour market, but of social exclusion, for the Union was to 'act not only in the interests of the employed but also of the unemployed and socially excluded' (CEC 1994a: 50); it thereby reflected a significant change made in the Maastricht Treaty in which the 'citizen' replaced the 'worker'.

Discursive Shifts

Globally, this was a period of considerable change: the collapse of the communist states; the 'ethnic cleansing' of the Balkan states; the continued decline of heavy industry; deepening economic, financial and cultural globalization, and of course, rising unemployment. It was also the period in which the European Community was enlarged, when it became the European Union and established a timetable for economic and monetary union. And, of course, it was the period in which the single market was completed. The concern with economic policy was broadened to address concerns regarding its effects and hence, social policy was greatly increased.

The dominant discourse of the period was political—the construction of the European Union itself—manifested primarily through the TEU, and developed further through the White Papers of *Growth, Social Policy* and *Education and Training*. There were three main areas of the Treaty that had a direct influence on the future development of the Fund: it enlarged and consolidated the competency for social policy; it gave new, albeit limited, competency within the field of education; and it replaced the previous concern with the worker for that of the citizen. The significant shift in the political competency of the European Union enabled a more complex reading of the critical problem of structural unemployment, such as that presented in the White Papers which stated clearly that social policy and economic policy were to go hand-in-hand. From within the new understanding of the complexity of unemployment, the Fund became far more flexible in the range of measures that it would support.

In this period the sub-discourse of human resources continued, in a somewhat subdued and taken-for-granted fashion that obscured the underlying discursive tension—a tension that existed between the dominant discourses of economic growth and political stability. This tension was centred on the threat to political stability caused by the social and material consequences of economic growth. This was the period in which the sub-discourses of social exclusion and pathologization were strengthened.

The strength of the sub-discourses of exclusion or cohesion is dependent on the specific weakness in the dominant discourse of political stability. For instance, the latest expansion of the Union included the relatively affluent Member States of Sweden, Finland and Austria— states that posed little economic-political threat. Despite the Structural Fund Reform's emphasis on social cohesion, tensions between Member States were of less immediate concern than the threat to stability and growth posed by unemployment and poverty within and across the Member States.

In addition to the overriding concern with unemployment and the related potential for social unrest, the construction of the sub-discourse of social exclusion was also related to the completion of the single market, the shift in emphasis away from the worker towards the unemployed, and the new competence in social policy.

The murmurs of pathologization that began in 1980, rumbled persistently throughout this period. Constructed primarily around 'disadvantaged youth', it was most visible within the weakening sub-discourse of human resources relative to the strengthening of that of social exclusion. When the sub-discourse of human resources is strong, emphasis is placed on vocational training related to the labour market; yet when the sub-discourse of social exclusion is strengthened, emphasis shifts onto the more nebulous and pathologizing areas of vocational guidance and counselling. Underpinning such a shift are repeated references to peoples' lack of basic skills, low education, lack of social skills and lack of motivation. Despite the fact that the sub-discourse of social exclusion is based on an understanding of multi-dimensional disadvantage, the sub-discourse of pathologization is based on the 'lack' of the individual person. The problem of unemployment had become less one of structural change to the labour market and more one of personal individual failure.

5 |

The ESF and Social Cohesion: 1997–2000

Political, Economic and Policy Context

Compared with the years of the previous chapter, 1997–2000 appeared, at first glance, to be less tumultuous. Yet they were deeply significant, for they not only consolidated developing trends towards monetary union, mobility and the role of the Commission, Parliament and Member States, but also prepared the way for the future expansion of the European Union.

The processes of globalization continued, and the role of the nation state became more and more questionable. The Multilateral Agreement on Investment (MAI) surfaced in 1998. Developed through the Organization for Economic Cooperation and Development (OECD), the MAI introduced a new set of investment rules that granted transnational corporations (TNCs) the right to buy, sell and move their operations wherever they wished around the world, without state regulation. It enabled TNCs to sue governments for any profits lost through any laws that discriminated against them; it increased the powers of TNCs and decreased those of the state (Rowan 1998). This led to a situation that I have described elsewhere as one in which:

> On one hand, the state can be seen as being left with the task of servicing the TNCs with an adequately educated, relatively healthy, compliant and flexible labour force. On the other hand, the state can be seen as mopping up the social and economic after-effects of TNC global power and national involvement: unemployment, poverty, social exclusion and possible unrest (Brine 1999b: 36).

Around the same time as the MAI surfaced, a crisis developed in the global finance system.[1] This began in south-east Asia and, throughout

---

1. A combination of government (especially Canada) and worldwide NGO (non-governmental organization) resistance led the OECD to halt the MAI talks in October 1998. However, in 2001 several governments reactivated the push for continuing talks within the World Trade Organization.

1997 and 1998, the resulting 'domino-effect' reverberated around the world causing panic and fear throughout the global economy.

As, on the one hand, the pressures of globalization impacted on the nation state, so, on the other hand, pressures within the state also threatened its stability; this was particularly so within the former Yugoslavia where disintegration led to the 'ethnic cleansing' atrocities within Kosovo, and the threat of 'Balkanization' spread to other multi-ethnic states. Beyond Kosovo the political tension and military action between the 'West' and Iraq continued.

From within the context of post-communism, increased globalization and Balkanization, this was a period of EU consolidation in which long-term goals such as the euro and the Schengen Agreement reached fruition, and the process of preparing for further enlargement began. There were five major developments during this time: the Schengen Agreement, the Amsterdam Treaty, the euro, the crisis surrounding the Commission, and the anticipated expansion of the Union.

The first, the Schengen Agreement, originally signed in June 1990 and finally incorporated into the Treaty of Amsterdam, reduced the internal border controls between all Member States except the UK, Ireland, and to a lesser extent, Denmark, thereby making the founding principle of 'free movement' far easier to implement (Swann 1992). As well as including the Schengen Agreement, the Amsterdam Treaty (CEC 1997b) expanded social policy (Sykes and Alcock 1998), introduced a chapter on employment (Pochet 1999), and introduced changes to the EU institutions themselves (Dinan 1999b; Moravcsik and Nicolaidis 1999). The third and perhaps most contentious major development was economic and monetary union, particularly the introduction from 1 January 1999 of the euro into the 11 participating Member States; those not included at the time were the UK, Sweden, Denmark and Greece.[2] The fourth development was that which erupted in 1998 when the European Parliament accused the Commission of fraud and the president, Jacques Santer, of seriously poor financial management (Dinan 1999b). The crisis culminated in March 1999 when the Commission was forced to resign and, subsequently, the majority reselected along with a new president, Romano Prodi. The new Commission

---

2.   The referendum in Denmark, held in October 2000, resulted in the decision not to join the euro. Equally contentious in the UK, heated discussions on the possibility of euro membership were a central feature in the approach to the 2001 general election.

quickly presented a White Paper in which it detailed its proposals for reform that included a complete review of its management and human resources policies, and the improvement of the financial management and accountability of the Commission itself. The final development was the projected expansion of the Union to include the applicant states of the Mediterranean and the Central and Eastern European Countries (CEEC).[3] These states were expected to make considerable demands upon the financial resources of the Union. The Commission's *Agenda 2000* (CEC 1997c), after a somewhat stormy passage (Galloway 1999), detailed the policy response to, and financial implications of, expansion. It was predicted that CEEC expansion would place an unprecedented demand on the Social Fund if economic and social cohesion were to be maintained.

Specifically with regard to policy, the first dominant theme was that of the European Employment Strategy which had begun with the White Paper on growth (CEC 1993b), was subsequently reaffirmed in the Amsterdam Treaty of June 1997 (CEC 1997b), and progressed further in the special Luxembourg Council on Employment held in November 1997 (CEC 1997a). It was finally adopted in the Council Resolution of 1999 that detailed the employment guidelines (CEC 1999b).

The second dominant theme, the enlargement of the Union to include the CEEC countries, was most clearly expressed in *Agenda 2000* (CEC 1997c), and subsequently agreed by the Berlin Council in March 1999, (CEC 1999c), and confirmed by the Intergovernmental Conference of Nice held in December 2000 (CEC 2000c).

The third dominant theme, the discursive shift from social exclusion to social cohesion is the concern of this chapter (Amin and Tommaney 1995). To recap, social cohesion—that is cohesion between the Member States and regions—had, since Article 130 of the SEA (CEC 1986b), been a major concern of the European Union, that was further strengthened through its inclusion in the TEU (CEC 1992a), where it became one of the three pillars of the European Union, along with economic and monetary union and the single market. The increased emphasis on cohesion was further consolidated in the Treaty of Amsterdam (CEC 1997b) and thereafter reiterated throughout the subsequent documents of the period.

---

3.   The CEEC applicant states are Bulgaria, the Czech Republic, Estonia, Hungary, Latvia, Lithuania, Poland, Romania, Slovakia and Slovenia, and the Mediterranean states are Cyprus and Malta.

During this period of the late 1990s, the Structural Funds were the largest means of redistribution after the Common Agricultural Policy (Kohli 1998). Approximately a quarter of the Structural Funds budget was distributed through the Social Fund—a far cry from its early position at the bottom of the pecking order. There was, however, only one key piece of ESF policy during this period—the 1999 Regulation that introduced the sixth reform of the Fund (CEC 1999a). Adopted towards the end of this period, the reform reflected the major concerns sketched above, and in doing so shifted away from its previous concern with social exclusion.

The chapter will begin by considering the Treaty of Amsterdam (CEC 1997b). It will be followed by a consideration of the employment strategy and will then focus on enlargement. The next section will be centred on the sixth reform (CEC 1999a) where it will explore the impact of the major forces upon it. The concluding section will focus on the discursive shifts that took place during this period.

The Treaty of Amsterdam 1997

With regard to the future development of the Social Fund, there were four significant amendments made by the Treaty of Amsterdam (CEC 1997b). First, the general strengthening of social (and environmental) concerns; second, the increased emphasis on education; third, the refocused concern with social cohesion; and fourth, the new title on employment.

The general strengthening of the social and environmental concerns of the Community were threaded throughout the Amsterdam Treaty, along with frequent demands related to mainstreamed gendered equal opportunities. The Amsterdam Treaty confirmed the Community's attachment to fundamental social rights and also the determination to:

> promote economic and social progress ... and within the context of ... reinforced cohesion ... to implement policies ensuring that advances in economic integration are accompanied by parallel progress in other fields (CEC 1997b: 7).

Article 2 listed many changes to the original Treaty that had established the European Community (CEC 1957). One of these promoted the 'development of the highest possible level of knowledge ... through a wide access to education and through its continuous updating' (CEC 1997b: 24). Most significant for the future development of the Fund was the Amsterdam Treaty's concern with cohesion and employment. Amending the TEU (CEC 1992a), the new Article B stated that the Union would 'promote economic and social progress and a high level of employment ... through the strengthening of economic and social cohesion' (CEC 1997b: 7). The concern with cohesion continued through the replacement of Article 2 of the Treaty of Rome (CEC 1957); it referred to:

> a high level of employment and of social protection, equality between men and women ... the raising of the standard of living and quality of life, and economic and social cohesion and solidarity among Member States (CEC 1997b: 24).

Moreover, the specific amendment to Article 130a of the 1957 Treaty declared that:

> In particular, the Community shall aim at reducing disparities between the levels of development of the various regions and the backwardness of the least favoured regions or islands, including rural areas (CEC 1997b: 41).

A great deal of subsequent policy made reference to this amended article.

The Treaty's strengthened concern with cohesion was reinforced by the new Title VIa on employment; it declared that the Member States and the Community would work towards:

> developing a coordinated strategy for employment and particularly for promoting a skilled, trained and adaptable workforce and labour markets responsive to economic change (CEC 1997b: 33).

Within this new title, the replaced Article 117 (of the Treaty of Rome), declared its objective to be the 'promotion of employment, improved living and working conditions ... and the development of human resources with a view to lasting high employment and the combating of exclusion' (p. 35). The following Article, 118, added that the Community would support Member States' activities concerning unemployed people, especially those that addressed the broader concerns of social exclusion. Further reinforcement was found in Article 118c that included employment and basic/advanced vocational training among its list of specific concerns. The Title on employment implemented the European Employment Strategy with its annual guidelines and its call for national action plans. It was, along with the strengthened discourse of social cohesion, to have a direct impact on the sixth reform of the

Social Fund (CEC 1999a). Whereas the Treaty of Rome (CEC 1957) had focused on free movement and the labour market, the Treaty of Amsterdam, from within the context of globalization and the techno-logical changes in production, was concerned with a proactive employment strategy that would address the problem of unemployment.

The Amsterdam Treaty also affected the numbering of the existing Articles related to the Fund, to education and to vocational training. The original ESF Articles 123, 124 and 125 became, respectively, 146, 147 and 148; Article 126 on the European dimension in education became Article 149; Article 127 (pre-Maastricht, Article 128) became Article 150; and the amended Article 130a on social cohesion became Article 158 (see Appendix 3).

Finally, looking towards the future enlargement of the Union, the Treaty of Amsterdam included a protocol in which it laid the ground for the subsequent reduction of Commissioners from each Member State; on CEEC enlargement there was to be one Commissioner per Member State.[4] It also stated that before exceeding 20 Member States, there would be a comprehensive review of the Treaties and the Community institutions.

The European Employment Strategy

Following on from the White Paper on growth (CEC 1993b), the Essen Council of 1994 and the White Paper on social policy (CEC 1994a) the Commission published a further paper related to unemployment—the *Action for Employment in Europe* (CEC 1996b). This referred to the problem of persistent unemployment and stressed the need for a medium and long-term coherent and all-embracing view of society. Again, education and training were seen as having a key role to play in developing the necessary skills for the labour market, in anticipating future needs, and in addressing the needs of young unemployed people through an 'integrated approach to training, social integration and guidance' (CEC 1996b: 25). There was, throughout the paper, an emphasis on the new technologies and the burgeoning information society, and it called upon the Structural Funds to respond to this. Moreover, yet again, this Paper re-emphasized the need for the Funds to be targeted upon the regions and social groups of greatest need—'three

4. Subsequently confirmed in the protocol on enlargement within the Treaty of Nice (CEC 2000c).

quarters of the Union's structural resources [were] concentrated on regions where two thirds of its unemployed [lived]' (p. 29). Significantly for the future development of the Fund, it called upon its imminent mid-term review to first, review the objectives in terms of their impact on employment, and second, to ensure that it mobilized local actors in the drive towards employment. The discourse in this paper's concern with unemployment is clearly that of human resources and economic growth. Furthermore, in this paper, exclusion is seen in its narrow context of exclusion from the labour market rather than the broader reading of multidimensional social exclusion expressed in the White Paper on social policy (CEC 1994a).

In the same year as the Amsterdam Treaty (CEC 1997b), a special Council meeting on employment was held at Luxembourg (CEC 1997a), where the Council concluded that the need for an employment strategy was considerable; it would 'mark a new departure in the thinking and action' on employment and it would 'create for employment, as for economic policy, the same resolve to converge towards jointly set, verifiable, regularly updated targets' (CEC 1997a: 7); over-optimistically, the Council spoke of 'turning back the tide of unemployment on a lasting basis' (p. 8).

The Luxembourg Council drew attention to the importance of preventative measures to reverse the trend of youth unemployment and long-term unemployment; it recommended that an individual's needs would be quickly identified and a tailor-made response would be made. It also recommended a change from passive to active employability measures which were to be linked to state benefit and training systems:

> Benefit and training systems—where that proves necessary—must be reviewed and adapted to ensure that they actively support employability and provide real incentives for the unemployed to seek and take up work or training opportunities (CEC 1997a: 12).

Note here the key reference to employability rather than actual employment. This strategy was to be built on the early identification of individual needs. Before being unemployed for six months, the young person was to be offered 'a new start in the form of training, retraining, work practice, a job or other employability measure' (CEC 1997a: 12).[5] The

---

5.   Within the UK, the demands specified by the Luxembourg Council, along with those of the subsequent Resolution (CEC 1999b), were replicated in the New Deal programme of the new Labour administration.

same options, plus individual vocational guidance, were to be offered to adults before they became unemployed for 12 months. However, the Council's greatest concern was shown for young people; they highlighted the 'very poor' employment prospects that existed, most particularly for those who left 'the school system without having acquired the aptitudes required for entering the job market' and, again moving into the area of compulsory education, called upon Member States to 'improve the quality of their school systems in order to reduce substantially the number of young people who drop out of the school system early' (CEC 1997a: 12). Note that, as part of the construction of the sub-discourse of pathologization, the young person is seen as lacking the necessary 'aptitudes' for entry to the job market. The Luxembourg Council also called explicitly upon the Social Fund to:

> serve employment needs wherever possible in the framework of the objectives assigned to them while respecting their *primary purpose, which is to enable regions lagging behind to catch up* (CEC 1997b: 10, emphasis added).

The interwoven sub-discourses of human resources and cohesion so clearly expressed in this sentence, subsequently dominated the sixth reform of the Fund.

The process towards a European employment strategy continued one year later through the meeting of the Vienna Council that led in the following year to the Council adopting a Resolution that established the employment guidelines (CEC 1999b). The Resolution Guideline reaffirmed employment as the top priority of the European Union, and stated that 'the ultimate objective ... [was] to arrive at a significant increase in the employment rate in Europe on a sustainable basis' (CEC 1999b: 8). Importantly, for the sub-discourse of social cohesion, the Guideline pointed to the need to recognize and support the regional and local role in implementing the employment strategy. It also referred to the Fund's 'positive contribution to the qualification of human resources', and confirmed that support for the employment strategy was to be strengthened in the next reform of the Fund. Finally, the Resolution reiterated the sentiments of the Luxembourg Council and restated the four pillars of the Employment Guidelines: improving employability, developing entrepreneurship, encouraging adaptability of businesses and their employees, and strengthening the policies for equal opportunities between women and men (CEC 1999b: 6). More specifically, here reiterating the Luxembourg Council's concerns over the quality of school education, it reaffirmed the options of 'training, retraining, work practice, a job or other employability measure' that were to be offered (CEC 1999b: 9). Picking up on the Council's remarks on state benefits, the Guidelines recommended that the benefit and tax system be 'refocused':

> Each Member State will review and, where appropriate, refocus its benefit and tax system and provide incentives for unemployed or inactive people to seek and take up work or measures to enhance their employability (CEC 1999b: 9).[6]

Finally, the Resolution highlighted those with 'particular difficulties' within the labour market and referred specifically to the ageing population (frequently linked with references to lifelong learning), 'the disabled' and 'ethnic minorities'. It called for 'a coherent set of policies promoting the integration of such groups and individuals into the world of work and combating discrimination' (CEC 1999b: 10). This was the first explicit non-gender specific reference to discrimination within the labour market. In line with the gender mainstreaming Resolution (CEC 1994b) discussed in the previous chapter, women were not included in the list of groups with 'particular difficulties', but in accordance with the four main pillars of the Guidelines, were referred to separately under the fourth pillar of 'strengthening equal opportunities'.

Towards the end of this period the Council held a special meeting at the Lisbon Council to agree a new strategic goal for the Union in order to 'strengthen employment, economic reform and social cohesion as part of a knowledge-based economy' (CEC 2000a; 1). The Council stated that unemployment still exceeded 15 million and remained a fundamental problem and 'long term structural unemployment and marked regional unemployment imbalances remained endemic in parts of the Union' (CEC 2000a: 2).[7] The aim of the strategy was to raise the employment rate from the then current rate of 61% to 70% by 2010, and to increase the number of women in employment from the then average of 51% to 60%. The strategy was focused on three approaches: the development of local learning centres, the promotion of basic skills that included those related to new technology, and the transparency of

6. Within the UK, for example, state benefits are linked to the Welfare to Work programme.

7. The 15 million unemployed of 2000 was only a slight reduction from the 1992 figure of 16 million (CEC 1992b), the 17 million of 1993 (CEC 1993b), and the predicted 18 million in 1995 (CEC 1994a).

qualifications. Four key areas were identified for future Council and Commission attention: improving employability and reducing skills gaps, giving higher priority to lifelong learning as a basic component of the European social model, increasing employment in the service sector (including personal services), and furthering all aspects of equal opportunities.

In addition to unemployment, the Council stated that the number of people living below the poverty line and in social exclusion was 'unacceptable' and that this must not be exacerbated by the new emphasis on a knowledge-based economy. Although it recommended that these concerns were to be coordinated into the Member State's national plans, it nevertheless called for the Commission to present a new initiative for cooperation in this field—that is, the concern with social exclusion and poverty were, in future, to be addressed by a separate programme, not the Social Fund. The Social Fund was henceforth to act exclusively as an instrument of labour market policy.

The sustained focus on employment during these years both reflected and constructed the resurgence of the sub-discourse of human resources and the decline of the sub-discourse of social exclusion that had preceded it. There is, throughout these documents on the employment strategy, no reference to social exclusion as such, nor to the broad social and economic consequences of unemployment—for either the individual or the Member State.

Enlargement of the Union

The Copenhagen Council in June 1993 agreed that the countries of Central and Eastern Europe that wished to join the Union would be able to, provided they satisfied the economic and political criteria. The Essen Council of 1994 requested a report that was duly submitted to the Madrid Council meeting in December 1995, where the accession negotiations were reaffirmed and the Commission requested to produce a more detailed report concerning the effects of enlargement on Community policies, particularly agricultural and structural policies. This led, two years later, to the most significant document on enlargement, *Agenda 2000* (CEC 1997c), in which the Commission outlined:

> in a single framework the broad perspectives for the development of the Union and its policies beyond the turn of the century, the horizontal issues related to enlargement, and the future financial framework beyond

2000 taking into account the prospect of an enlarged Union (CEC 1997c: 11).

Two years later the Berlin Council (CEC 1999c), reached an overall agreement on the policies and financial framework contained in the document that had clearly expressed the importance of enlargement:

> It is expected to bring major political benefits to the Union and to peace and security in Europe. In the economic field too, important benefits are expected, but problems, related to adjustment strains from the developing integration process, will also have to be addressed, especially since acceding countries are at a lower level of economic development, while they are still undergoing transition towards a market economy (CEC 1997c: 95).

Along with the economic and political effects and the accompanying 'adjustment strains', it was further acknowledged that enlargement would bring increased heterogeneity. Indeed,

> The integration of new members will be a complex task. It will pose a major challenge to the Union, its policies and its cohesion, while it is likely to put a strain on its resources. The objective must be to ensure that the full potential of enlargement is developed to strengthen the European model, namely a Europe built on a set of values shared by all its societies and combining the characteristics of democracy with those of an open economy underpinned by market forces, internal solidarity and cohesion (CEC 1997c: 95).

Enlargement was expected to have a huge impact: 'the number of applicant countries and the differences between them are greater than ever before, and they will all be net recipients of Community funds'— hence the need for a tight budgetary framework (CEC 1997c: 11), for the new members were likely to 'draw important amounts from Community programmes and structural funds' (p. 100). A prime concern within this process was the 'unacceptably high rates of unemployment and social exclusion which tear at the very fabric of society' (p. 13). Consequently, the report predicted that social policy would have to address the 'acute social problems' including unemployment and the 'insufficiently developed vocational training networks' of the CEEC states (p. 99). Alongside enlargement itself the Commission foresaw significant demographic changes taking place in which, over the next 25 years, the number of people aged over 60 would grow by 37 million, whereas the working population would decrease by 13 million. This prediction further strengthened the 'need to increase the qualifications of young people and to offer the perspective of a full-length working life through continuous learning' (p. 14). These observations were to have a considerable effect on both the general distribution and the specific targeting of the Social Fund. Moreover, *Agenda 2000* pointed out that future reforms of the Structural Funds would need to 'deepen the commitment to economic and social cohesion' (p. 14).

Writing specifically about the Structural Funds, *Agenda 2000* stated that, 'for reasons of visibility and efficiency', the existing seven objectives should be reduced to three: two regional objectives and a horizontal objective for human resources. The objective 1 regions faced the 'most serious difficulties in terms of income, employment, the productive system and infrastructure' (p. 22) with an average level of unemployment 60% higher than the Community average. The number of people eligible for assistance under objective 1 was predicted to rise from 94 million to 200 million. *Agenda 2000* advocated that two-thirds of the total amount of the Structural Funds should be allocated to the strictly determined objective 1 regions (that is, those regions with a GDP less than 75% of the Community average). The objective 2 regions were those that were 'undergoing economic change (in industry or services)' and included rural areas, areas dependent on the fishing industry and urban areas in difficulty—all areas that 'were facing structural problems and ... a high rate of unemployment or depopulation' (CEC 1997c: 23). Within the objective 1 and 2 regions, objective 3 was to be used for access to employment, lifelong learning, and the promotion of local employment including territorial employment pacts.

While the resources of the Structural Funds were targeted far more closely onto the objective 1 and 2 regions, the Commission also pointed to the considerable problem that still existed in the non-priority regions where almost one-fifth of the population lived in areas with an unemployment rate above the Community average; it declared that 'youth unemployment is still over 30%. In some urban areas, unemployment ranges from 30 to 50%' (CEC 1997c: 23). The remaining non-priority regions were to be covered by the new horizontal objective 3—or, more precisely, by what remained of objective 3 after its allocation to the priority areas. The new objective 3 was to be sufficiently flexible so as to reflect a variety of systems, approaches and levels of development in the Member States; it was to be used in conjunction with Member States' own national policies and it was to promote activity in those areas that would complement the European Employment Strategy guidelines: first, accompanying economic and social changes; second, lifelong education and training systems; third, active labour market policies to fight unemployment; and fourth, combating social exclusion.

Agenda 2000 acknowledged that 'enlargement [would] highlight the importance of social cohesion' (p. 99), and hence enhance the role of social policy. It stated that:

> reinforcement of economic and social cohesion is, and will remain, one of the fundamental pillars of the European Union, together with the single market and economic and monetary union, [and moreover] cohesion policies will be reinforced in their current basic principles and will be adapted to become more exacting, particularly through measures required to improve concentration of effort, effectiveness, monitoring and simplification (CEC 1997c: 109).

The Structural Funds themselves were to address issues of cohesion, most specifically through their direct contribution to each region's own regeneration programme.

Two years after the publication of *Agenda 2000*, in March 1999 the Berlin Council (CEC 1999c) reached an overall agreement on both its policies and its financial framework. The Berlin Council assumed that the accession of the new Member States would begin in 2002, and that the financial framework would cover the years 2000 to 2006; a 'central plank' of this framework would be the Structural Funds and the Cohesion Fund. The Berlin Council reaffirmed that the Structural Funds, in their new streamlined guise of three objectives, would be concentrated on the areas of greatest need. It also agreed the financial allocation across the seven-year period and between the three objectives: 69.7% was to be allocated to the top priority objective 1 regions, 11.5% to the objective 2 regions, and the remaining 12.3% to objective 3.[8] It also reaffirmed that objective 1 would 'promote the development and structural adjustment of regions whose development [was] lagging behind'; objective 2 would 'support the economic and social conversion of areas facing structural difficulties'—these would not exceed 18% of the Union's population. In contrast to the earlier *Agenda 2000* document, the Berlin Council stated that objective 3 would only apply outside the objective 1 regions, and would be distributed to each Member State on the basis of the severity of their

---

8. In addition to the sums given to the three objectives a further 5% was allocated to the Community Initiatives, 1% to innovative actions and technical assistance, and the remaining 0.5% to recipients listed under 'particular situations'.

unemployment and social exclusion, the levels of education and training and the participation of women in the labour market. Most specifically, objective 3 would 'lend support to the adaptation and modernisation of policies and systems of education, training and employment' (CEC 1999c: 6).

Throughout the first 20 or so years of the Fund, Article 125 of the EEC Treaty had demanded that a retrained person would work in a direct training-related occupation for at least six months following training. The third reform of the Fund (CEC 1983a), removed this requirement, and five years later the fourth reform broadened the definition of vocational training to include 'any measure aimed at providing the skills necessary to carry out one or more specific types of employment' (CEC 1988a: 22). The Berlin Council, in directing objective 3 towards the support of the policies and systems of education, training and employment, significantly broadened the actions available under the Fund and targeted it more closely onto the regions of greatest need, thereby ensuring greater flexibility within Member State national and regional policies and framing the sub-discourse of human resources within that of social cohesion.

In December 2000 the IGC of Nice led to the Treaty (CEC 2000c) that reaffirmed the decision that, from the end of 2002, the Union was to be in a position to accept those applicant Member States that were ready. The Treaty, focused primarily on the institutional and representational changes related to enlargement was firmly located within the dominant discourse of political stability and the related sub-discourse of social cohesion.

Reform of the Structural Funds: 1999

The sixth reform of the Fund cannot be considered without close attention to the earlier Regulation of June 1999 that reformed the Structural Funds themselves (CEC 1999d). The reform of the Structural Funds was directly related to the post-Amsterdam Article 158 of the amended 1957 Treaty;[9] it confirmed the Community's need to strengthen economic and social cohesion, and most particularly to reduce the 'disparities between the levels of development of the various regions and the backwardness of the least-favoured regions or islands'.

9.   Referred to as Article 130a in the Treaty of Amsterdam and the Single European Act (CEC 1986b).

Indeed, the Structural Funds reform demanded a three-yearly report on the actual progress made towards economic and social cohesion.

Confirming the recommendation of *Agenda 2000* (CEC 1997c), the number of objectives were reduced from seven to three, and most importantly it confirmed the redefinition of the objectives as:

> objective 1: to promote 'the development and structural adjustment of regions whose development is lagging behind';
> objective 2: to promote the 'economic and social conversion of areas facing structural difficulties';
> objective 3: to adapt and modernize 'policies and systems of education, training and employment' (CEC 1999d: 1).

With specific regard to objective 3, the Structural Funds reform followed the decision of the Berlin Council and stated that objective 3 would in future be limited to the non-objective 1 regions. Moreover, with its much enhanced flexibility, Member States would be able to use objective 3 for 'all measures [that promoted] human resources' (p. 7). In defining objectives 1 and 2 the Structural Funds gave precise details on the qualification criteria, measured against the percentages of GDP and the newly introduced Nomenclature of Territorial Statistical Units (NUTS). Objective 2 areas were to be those undergoing socio-economic change in the industrial and service sectors, declining rural areas, urban areas in difficulty or depressed areas dependent on fisheries. Referring specifically to urban areas 'in difficulty' the Reform pointed to high population density, a high rate of long-term unemployment, high levels of poverty and low levels of education. However, the requirements for gaining objective 2 status were stringent. From the Structural Funds budget, 11.5% (€22.5bn) would, as stated previously, be allocated to objective 2 as compared to 69.7% (€135.9bn) for objective 1 regions, and 12.3% for objective 3 (€24.05bn)—albeit, the majority of which would be allocated to objective 2 regions.

Along with the expected reference to the mainstreamed concern with gendered equal opportunities, and the new reference to environmental factors, the Structural Funds Regulation stated for the first time that:

> the Funds' operations may also make it possible to combat any discrimination on the grounds of race, ethnic origin, disability or age by means in particular of an evaluation of needs, financial incentives and an enlarged partnership (CEC 1999d: 2).

Thus within the dominant framing of economic and social cohesion and maximum national/regional flexibility, some of the earlier concerns of social exclusion were restated as forms of discrimination. Discrimination did not, however, unlike social exclusion, make any reference to poverty; nor was it linked to long-term unemployment and its multi-dimensional material, social and political consequences. Most specifically, the Structural Funds reform stated that the Social Fund's task was to respond to, and implement, the European Employment Strategy.

The Structural Funds reform (CEC 1999d) also referred to the responsibilities of the Commission and the Member States; these were 'precisely defined' for each stage of the programming, monitoring and evaluation process; *ex ante*, mid-term and *ex post*. At each stage the effectiveness of the Fund's operations was to be measured, first, against their impact on the social cohesion goals expressed in Article 158 of the revised Treaty (CEC 1997b); and second, for their impact on the priorities listed in the Member State's development plan and Community Support Framework (Appendix 4).[10] Indeed, monitoring was seen as a clear way of making the Funds more effective. In line with the tighter focusing of the Funds and the move towards their more efficient use, the Structural Funds Regulation clarified the thorny question of additionality by stating that:

> In order to achieve a genuine economic impact, the appropriations of the Funds may not replace public or other equivalent structural expenditure by the Member State (CEC 1999d: 14).[11]

To this end, the Member State was to agree with the Commission its own level of 'structural expenditure' over the programming period. The demand on Member States, in respect of plans, programming documents and Community Support Frameworks, was extensive and was carefully detailed in the Regulation. Moreover, in relation to objective 3 it stated that the Member State's plans were to be consistent with its national plan for implementing the European Employment Strategy. Despite the flexibility given to Member States in their use of the Structural Funds, and despite the Member State's responsibility for implementation and evaluation, the Regulation nevertheless demanded a great deal of background information and detailed action plans from

10. This increased complexity of the Structural Funds was reflected in the Regulations glossary of the language used (CEC 1999d: 12-13), the key sections of which are reproduced in Appendix 4.

11. For further discussion of the concept of additionality, see Barnett and Boorooah (1995) and Harrop (1996).

Member States which were then to be agreed with the Commission. It also laid down the detailed procedures for the financial management of and accountability of the Funds.

Sixth Reform of the ESF: The 1999 Regulation

The month following the Regulation on the Structural Funds (CEC 1999d), a further Regulation (CEC 1999a) introduced the sixth reform of the Social Fund. The sixth reform reflected the dominant themes of the period: the overriding concern with employment and the regional redistribution of resources to accommodate the predicted needs of CEEC and Mediterranean enlargement. In its preamble it detailed the new enlarged scope of the Fund—namely, that it would combat 'all forms of discrimination and inequalities in connection with the labour market' (CEC 1999a: 5). Unlike previous reforms of the Fund, the sixth reform did not add any further clarification to the details specified in the Structural Funds Regulation (CEC 1999d).

The sixth reform reaffirmed the demands of the Employment Strategy—that the Fund be related not only to the social and economic policies of the Commission but also to the priorities of Member States' national action plans. It further stated that arrangements *may* be introduced that would allow non-governmental organizations to 'gain simple and rapid access to the Fund support for operations concerned with combating social exclusion' (p. 6). The main concern of this reform, however, was employment; combating and preventing unemployment now replaced the earlier primary concern with training. The first of the five activities of the reformed Fund was:

> developing and promoting active labour market policies to combat and prevent unemployment, to prevent both women and men from moving into long-term unemployment, to *facilitate* the reintegration of the long-term unemployed into the labour market, and to support the occupational integration of young people or persons returning to the labour market after a period of absence (CEC 1999a: 6, emphasis added).

The prime activity was one of facilitation and support. The second activity was to 'promote equal opportunities for all in accessing the labour market, with particular emphasis on those exposed to social exclusion' (p. 6). The third, the promotion and improvement of training, education, counselling and lifelong learning activities related to *employability*, and the fourth was related to job creation. Finally, the fifth activity of the Fund was that related specifically to women's participation in the labour market and to vertical and horizontal gendered segregation.

From within the context of the five activities of the Fund, the Reform detailed the eligible measures that were more wide ranging and flexible than ever before. The first measure was education and vocational training; to include apprenticeships, basic skills and, for people with disabilities, 'rehabilitation in employment'. The significance of the prime reference to education reflected the demand made in the Resolution on employment guidelines that Member States should 'improve the quality of their school systems' (CEC 1999b: 10). The sixth reform went on to state that 'education and vocational training' should include 'vocational training equivalent to compulsory schooling'. Significantly, the reference was to the much broader concept of education and not, as previously, to the more narrowly defined vocational education. The second measure referred, as in the previous reform, to employment aids and aids for self-employment. The third and fourth measures were new: the third supported activities in the fields of research, science and technology, especially those related to post-graduate training and the training of managers and technicians in these fields; the fourth covered the development of new sources of employment, including the social economy. The social economy was defined as that area of new employment that included cooperatives and other not-for-profit measures such as those where people were trained and then subsequently employed in community enterprises.

The range of measures eligible under the Fund were much increased and hence allowed the Member State, at national and regional level, increased flexibility in its use—provided it was within the broad scope of combating and preventing unemployment. The sixth reform was no longer predominantly concerned with training measures that would address the situation of unemployment, but with a far wider range of activities that would *prevent* unemployment as well as combat it; these proactive measures included vocational training within schools,[12] activities within the social economy, and postgraduate training in the sciences. Moreover, in order to increase their effectiveness, the Fund also supported the training of trainers, improved the access of those in

12. The possibility of the Fund being used for vocational training within schools was first introduced for objective 1 areas in the fourth reform of 1988 (CEC 1988a), and extended to objective 3 in the fifth reform of 1993 (CEC 1993a).

work to training and qualifications, and developed systems that would anticipate changes in employment and qualification needs. At the same time the Fund continued to fund accompanying measures such as care for dependants, 'socio-educational development', general awareness-raising and publicity activities.

Given the fact that, as confirmed in the reform of the Structural Funds, the Social Fund was to be tightly targeted onto the areas of greatest need, the sixth reform produced a highly flexible Fund for use within the national employment strategies of Member States. Beneath the targeted, streamlined objectives, and the measures for combating unemployment, the most significant change was the increased underlying concern with the *prevention* of unemployment, as illustrated through the emphasis on the social economy and various new forms of employment. Preventative measures had first been introduced, for priority objective 1 areas only, in the fourth reform (CEC 1988a) and subsequently extended to other areas through the redefined objective 4 introduced in the fifth reform (CEC 1993a) in which training was provided for people employed in work of a vulnerable nature.

With the sixth reform, the Fund became the key instrument within the European Strategy for Employment, channelling funds to those regions of current and future Member States in greatest need. Earlier struggles between the Commission and the Member States over who would control the Fund, have, in the face of globalization, Balkanization and enlargement, led to a certain degree of shared power, of tenuous balance and compromise. The Fund became a proactive instrument of European employment and labour market strategy; in its considerably increased flexibility it gave Member States maximum scope for using it more freely as part of their own national employment strategy.

Discursive Shifts

The enlargement of the Union was seen as a major challenge to its cohesion; consequently, the focus for the redistributive actions of the Fund was shifted from the citizen of the fifth reform (and worker of the previous reforms) to the Member State/region of the sixth. As in the early years of the European Economic Community, stability between the Member States and their regions was the prime concern, and as then, such stability was strengthened through the over-riding dominant discourse of economic growth that remained as intertwined as ever with the equally dominant discourse of political stability. However, unlike the 1960s and 1970s the solution in this period was no longer located in the simplistically straightforward relationship between vocational training and the labour market; rather, the emphasis at the turn of the century was on the state of unemployment itself and the need to both combat and prevent it through active labour market measures. Therefore, despite the strong resurgence of the sub-discourse of human resources (particularly within the sixth reform), there was within it a significant discursive shift: the centrality of training was displaced and distanced from the needs of the labour market. The focus of attention was unemployment, but unlike in the previous period, there was scarcely any mention at all of the broader social, economic and even political consequences of long-term unemployment. Indeed, the emphasis, as in the Structural Funds Reform (CEC 1999d), on discrimination, separated the 'disadvantage' of particular social groups away from poverty and its associated connection with the consequences of economic growth—a discursive shift that could be seen as a pathologization at the social level that mirrored that previously constructed around the unemployed individual.

Within the sixth reform of the Fund, the sub-discourse of human resources was apparent in the redefined relationship of the three objectives to the European Employment Strategy. However, the sub-discourse of social cohesion was evident throughout the entire revised structural framework of the Fund, its increased flexibility and its intended effectiveness as a proactive instrument of EU policy. While there were discursive tensions between the sub-discourses of human resources and social cohesion, the latter was dominant. The flexibility of the Fund and its redistributive function towards the Member States and regions in greatest need, was paramount and the concern with employment strategies could only take place once the redistribution of resources had been achieved and the political demands of social cohesion met.

In the latter years of the twentieth century, the dominant discourses of economic growth and political stability remained in a state of intertwined tension that in many ways resembled those of the mid-century. The prospect of the considerably enlarged Union created concerns similar to those that faced the original six. Again, the noisier discourse of economic growth was in fact subservient, or contributory to, the over-riding dominant discourse of political stability. At the same time, at both times, political stability was reliant on economic growth. Hence, while the strengthened and resurgent sub-discourse of human resources was clearly linked to the European Economic Strategy and the dominant discourse of economic growth, it was constructed through the dominant discourse of political stability.

6 |

The Flexible Fund

The discursive analysis of the Social Fund has been focused on the policy documents themselves rather than the processes of policy making or implementation. These documents, freely available within the public domain, are the textual representation of policy at that particular moment. At the same time, however, they are the process by which discourses are constructed—discourses that are the systematic and regular 'corpus of statements' referred to by Kendall and Wickham (1999). As such they are instruments of power that discursively express and construct the European Union itself.

There are, as explained in Chapter 1, two approaches to this discursive analysis of the Social Fund. The first is concerned with changes in structure, practice and its relationship to other policies and the construction of the Union; an approach developed throughout the preceding chapters. The second approach is that which is concerned with the Fund as an instrument of redistribution to disadvantaged social groups and regions. Both approaches are further explored within this chapter that focuses primarily on the Fund as both a proactive instrument of policy and as an instrument of redistribution.

This concluding chapter draws together the themes and theoretical findings of the previous chapters. From within the overall context of the construction of the European Union, it argues that, paradoxically, the consistent feature of the Fund is its flexibility—a flexibility seen most immediately in the changing fundable measures that it has, at different times, supported (detailed throughout Chapters 2–5), but also, as shown below, in its discursive flexibility.

The context for the Fund's flexibility has been both global and European, political, economic and social. Throughout the latter half of the twentieth century and into the twenty-first, the impact of globalization and demography, and the technological changes in production have had a damaging effect on employment—a situation further affected by the construction of the EU and, most particularly, the single market. Within the European Union, periods of enlargement, increases in unemployment and the fear of unrest caused by social and regional disadvantage have all made further demands on its flexibility.

The main shifts of flexibility, grouped into four periods, are indicated by the titles of Chapters 2–5. The first, 1957–77, was focused on the labour market and the worker. The second, 1978–88, was dominated by technological change and the rise of unemployment. The third, 1989–96, saw the growing concern with social exclusion, and the fourth, 1997–2000, was, in the light of further expansion, focused on social cohesion between the regions and Member States.

The first section of this chapter is focused on the Fund as an instrument of VET policy and, primarily from within the dominant discourse of economic growth, on the related sub-discourses of human resources and pathologization. The second section focuses on the major tension that, from within the dominant discourses of political stability and economic growth, has framed one particular aspect of the Fund's flexibility—that is, the tension between the Commission and the individual Member State. In doing so, it also explores the effectiveness of the Fund as an instrument of policy and redistribution. The chapter concludes by reconsidering the role of the Fund in its relationship to the dominant discourses of economic growth and political stability.

The Fund as an Instrument of VET Policy

The sub-discourses of human resources and pathologization have been constructed primarily from within the dominant discourse of economic growth. They are, nevertheless, affected by the shifts in the dominant discourse of political stability, particularly the shifting emphasis between the sub-discourses of social exclusion and social cohesion. Within the strengthening sub-discourse of social cohesion, that of human resources also grows stronger, whereas, when the sub-discourse of social exclusion strengthens, the VET emphasis turns to pathologization.

There was a shift in the development of the Fund from the early concern with the geographical and occupational flexibility of the worker towards the post-Fordist demands for flexibility between employment and unemployment. While present throughout the six reforms of the Fund, the sub-discourse of human resources has changed significantly from its original concern with the needs of the labour market, to its latest positioning with regard to the pathologization of 'the unemployed' and 'employability'.

As early as the first reform of 1971 (CEC 1971a, b), reference was made to the social consequences of economic practices and to the particular training needs of young people (explicitly not school-leavers). The second reform of 1977 (CEC 1977a) directed the Fund towards 'the unemployed', and the third reform (CEC 1983a, d) removed the direct relationship between training and subsequent employment. However, in 1988 the Regulation combining the Structural Funds (CEC 1988e) consolidated the shift away from training related to employment towards that centred on unemployment and 'employability'. Furthermore, the Structural Funds Regulation declared the aim of the Social Fund as one that would combat long-term unemployment and encourage the integration of young people into the labour market. Along with the change in emphasis, there was a change in the supportable measures themselves; the related fourth reform of 1988 (CEC 1988a) widened the definition of vocational training and introduced the need for vocational guidance.

Despite the group-based analysis of disadvantage that lies at the centre of the sub-discourse of social exclusion, the foci of VET remained firmly on the individual and not the group. This individualization was particularly evident in the redefinition of the VET curricula where the sub-discourses of social exclusion and pathologization emerged to challenge the existing dominant sub-discourse of human resources. This challenge continued throughout the period covered by the fifth reform of 1993, where the definition of vocational training was extended and the measure of 'counselling' introduced. Counselling, along with vocational guidance, was given priority over and above vocational training itself—the sub-discourse of pathologization over that of human resources. Finally, in the light of further EU expansion and the renewed strength of the sub-discourse of social cohesion, the sub-discourse of human resources was, within the sixth reform of 1999, once again strengthened; only this time it was related more to the sub-discourse of social cohesion and the dominant discourse of political stability rather than to that of economic growth.

This VET discourse of pathologization constructed the unemployed person as lacking confidence, lacking work experience, lacking motivation and lacking adequate education. In thus laying the blame onto the unemployed individual the discourse effectively deflected attention away from the economic, societal and political causes of unemployment. The construction of the sub-discourse of pathologization could be traced through the changes in Fundable measures described above—that is, the priority given through the fourth, fifth and sixth reforms to vocational guidance and counselling. These changes reflected the European and global economic and political context which pointed to continued high unemployment and economic and social instability. These were the years of increased economic globalization and rising unemployment, the collapse of communism and the reunification of Germany, the expansion of the European Union and the threat of a 'dual society'. At that time there was also a perceived shift from a Fordist to a post-Fordist economy, a new economy with an emphasis on employment flexibility, technological literacy, transferable generic skills, and an increased insecurity for all workers—most especially the 'low- and under-educated'. With such a high probability of unemployment, and low probability of training leading to employment, it was not surprising that training became divorced from employment, nor that 'the unemployed' rather than the economy or the state would be blamed for their continued unemployment.

Between Growth and Stability: The Flexible Fund

This study of the Social Fund has been based on an analysis of the shifting discourses discernible within it. Such discourses are certainly not static, either in time, in relation to other discourses, or in their positioning as dominant, sub, or reverse. The account of the discursive tensions surrounding the Fund, highlighted its central location at the interface of economic, social and vocational training policies.

The first glimmerings of what would become the sub-discourse of social exclusion were evident within the third reform of 1983; this built on the earlier reform's concern with disadvantaged social groups, especially women 'returners' and unemployed young people. Further strengthened in the fourth reform of 1988, social exclusion emerged most strongly in the fifth reform of 1993 as the Fund responded to the main concern of unemployment. This reflected a period of transition and struggle in which the Fund was shifted away from its focus on employment to one where the main concern was unemployment. And, most importantly, unemployment was seen as part of a much larger and far more complex situation of poverty and exclusion from social as well as economic life. However, in the sixth reform of 1999, the sub-discourse of social exclusion was itself superseded by that of social cohesion, and moreover, of a return of the sub-discourse of human resources—albeit reworked to include that of pathologization. There is then no distinct binary between the discourse of human resources and the discourse of social exclusion; they are like two wavy lines that originate from a common source, cross over each other and sometimes even merge. At the turn of the century, the sub-discourse of social cohesion and that of human resources were directly related to the dominant discourse of political stability.

The first traces of the sub-discourse of social cohesion were evident in the period following the second reform of 1977. This followed the adoption of the ERDF in 1975. With the subsequent integration in the early 1980s of the less affluent states of Greece, Spain and Portugal, the concern with regional imbalance was further strengthened within the third and fourth reforms. Most particularly, the objectives of the fourth reform targeted the Fund onto those regions of greatest need. The integration in 1995 of the wealthier states of Austria, Finland and Sweden made no such demands on the Fund, and the sub-discourse of social cohesion remained weakened but fundamentally unchanged throughout the period of the fifth reform. However, the imminent expansion to include the CEEC and Mediterranean applicant states, reminiscent of the integration of Spain, Portugal and Greece, provoked within the sixth reform such a renewed strengthening of the sub-discourse of social cohesion that it came to dominate that of social exclusion.

In the approach to the latest, and by far the largest, process of enlargement, the sub-discourse of human resources has been strengthened within both the dominant discourses of economic growth and political stability. When the political discourse is most closely targeted onto stability between Member States and regions, it grows more reliant on the human resource sub-discourse of economic growth. On the other hand, during periods of inter-state stability, the inequalities across the Member States are more evident and the political discourse of exclusion is then strengthened and draws, from within the discourse of economic growth, on the sub-discourse of pathologization.

The Commission, the Fund and the Member State

Within the complex and often contradictory European project there are a variety of positions held by Member State governments, ranging from profound federalism to loose intergovernmentalism.

The fundamental dominant political discourse on the construction of the Union does not express a single straightforward progressive goal, but rather a woven thread of many strands with many snags and even the occasional tangled knot to hinder even the development of compromise that epitomizes this discourse. From within this context, the discourse of economic growth is sometimes opposed to that of political stability and sometimes an integral part of it—its position along the continuum reflects the particular political stance of the Union itself; on the one hand the discourse of economic growth leads in a fairly straightforward way to a free trading agreement (albeit a complex one), whereas on the other hand, as the first president of the Commission, Hallstein, is reported to have said, economic growth is most importantly a means of attaining the long-term goal of deeper political union (McAllister 1997). The political/economic tension was most clearly expressed in the disagreements between President Jacques Delors and the UK Prime Minister Margaret Thatcher, and has erupted more recently in the heated debates surrounding Schengen and the euro.[1]

The dominance of the discourse of economic growth has been struggled over throughout the entire lifespan of the EEC/EU; a similar struggle has centred on the dominant political discourse, especially that which has centred on federalism and nation state sovereignty, and more recently, on the challenge presented by the sub-discourse of social exclusion.

The sub-discourses of social exclusion and social cohesion represent shifts in the dominant discourse of political stability; they exist in a state of tension with the sub-discourses of human resources and pathologization more clearly located within the dominant discourse of economic growth. In the run-up to Maastricht, and increasingly thereafter, the extension of social policy led to a decrease in the strength of the sub-discourse on human resources, and an increase in the strength of the sub-discourses of social cohesion and social exclusion as the

---

1.   Within the UK these debates are found both between and within political parties, the government and among the general public.

Fund was directed towards both long-term unemployed adults and young people, and towards the most underdeveloped regions. Most particularly, the Social Fund has operated at the interface of the economic, social and political discourses.

The tension between the Commission and the Member State governments that has revolved around the construction of the European Union has also focused on the role that the Fund has played within it; the Commission wanted the Fund to be a proactive instrument within European labour market policy; the Member States wanted to use their 'allocation' freely as part of their national policies. This basic tension led, in part, to the regular changes in the reforms of the Fund—a steady double-edged process of compromise in which the Member States were given more freedom to use the Fund as they wished—provided it was within the agreed parameters set by the Commission. The sub-discourses of social exclusion and social cohesion, while not highlighted as such, are nevertheless evident throughout this section.

The first reform of 1971 (CEC 1971a, b) strengthened the administration of the Fund and gave the Commission a greater consolidating and coordinating role whereby the Member State's free use of the Fund was framed by the Commission's guidelines and priorities as it was targeted onto specific occupational groups. In the second reform of 1977 (CEC 1977a) the Commission's powers of coordination and control were further strengthened, and consequently they used the Guidelines to target the Fund onto the growing numbers of unemployed people. The second reform also saw the sub-discourse of social cohesion being formed as the Fund was targeted onto the most under-developed regions. Yet from within these policy constraints the Member States were given greater freedom to use the resources of the Fund within their national policies. They were also given greater administrative responsibilities. In 1983, the third reform (CEC 1983a) continued this balance between Commission 'guidance' and Member State freedom, as it targeted the Fund more tightly onto particular social groups, especially young and adult unemployed people, and on those regions in greatest need. With the third reform, the Fund became a far more proactive instrument, yet, from within Commission-defined limits, the potential for Member States to use the Fund within their national programmes was further increased.

The fourth reform of 1988 (CEC 1988a) was most significant with regard to the Commission/Member State tension. The Commission built on the previous system of priorities and guidelines to introduce a new structure of objectives through which the Fund was more firmly targeted onto the regions of greatest need and onto young and adult unemployed people. Along with the introduction of the Community Support Framework (CSF), the Commission's own 'Initiatives', and the move within the prioritized objective 1 regions towards preventative measures, the proactive potential of the Fund was greatly increased. The fourth reform also introduced the concept of 'partnership' whereby the Commission and the Member States were to agree, within the CSF, the Fund's priorities for each individual Member State, thereby consolidating the principle of diversity among, and autonomy within, the Member States. Member State administrative responsibilities were again increased.

These trends were continued in the fifth reform of 1993 (CEC 1993a). Although decision-making powers continued to be devolved to Member States, the centralized framework for the Fund was further strengthened and its proactive potential considerably increased. The objectives were redefined with further emphasis placed on unemployment and social exclusion. The preventative measures introduced in the fourth reform were expanded along with increased flexibility in the range of measures that it would support.

The focus on flexibility continued in the sixth reform of 1999 (CEC 1999a), where the Commission framework guided the newly streamlined three objectives of the Fund most directly onto the regions of greatest need and, moreover, from within this tightly focused redistribution, extended the actual range of measures that it would support. At the same time, the consistent shift of administrative responsibilities to Member States continued, with the result that administrative, financial and managerial tasks were now ostensibly 'shared' between them and the Commission.

At the European level the Fund has steadily, but stealthily, developed into a central instrument of European (un)employment and VET-related policy. More openly, it has continued to operate as an instrument of redistribution, primarily between Member States and regions (cohesion) but also at times of inter-state stability, with regard primarily to disadvantaged social groups, unemployment and poverty (exclusion).

The persistent Commission/Member State tension is related to the basic question concerning the extent to which the Fund is primarily an instrument of redistribution or a proactive instrument of policy. At different times, determined by the particularities of the dominant discourses of political stability and economic growth, decisions on the focus of redistribution have changed, yet the move towards making it a more proactive instrument has steadily continued.

In the first instance, in line with the dominant discourse of economic growth, the Fund operated as a proactive instrument of labour market policy where the main concern was with the 'flexible worker' and 'his' geographical and occupational mobility. In the move towards the single market and, with the fourth reform of 1988 (CEC 1988a), it became an instrument of social cohesion, where the main concern, still focused on the 'flexible worker' was related to his and her flexibility between employment and unemployment. Following the TEU (CEC 1992a), amid the surge in social policy, the focus shifted from the worker to the unemployed person as it became an instrument for addressing unemployment and social exclusion.

At the turn of the century, the expansion of the Union to include the CEEC and Mediterranean applicant states has provoked important changes in the use of the Fund. First and foremost the sub-discourse of social cohesion dominated—and the Fund's role as a proactive instrument of redistribution was considerably strengthened. Second, it was firmly linked to the new European Employment Strategy (CEC 1997a) thereby reinforcing its role as a proactive instrument of labour market policy. Third, the range of supportable measures were broadened thereby enabling Member States to use it more freely as part of their national strategy. Finally, the sub-discourse of social exclusion was much weakened—a shift reinforced by the decision of the Lisbon Council of 2000 to develop a new programme that would address the problems of social exclusion and poverty, which would leave the Fund to operate exclusively within the sub-discourse of human resources, as an instrument of labour market policy.

The redistributive focus of the Fund to combat social exclusion has declined, whereas that to maintain peace, cooperation and stability between Member States has increased. Moreover, within this sub-discourse of social cohesion, there has been an increased emphasis on redistribution, on the material inequality of Member States and regions, rather than the inequality of social groups. Member State/regional inequality represents more of a threat to the stability of the Union than that of unemployed, socially excluded people. However, while the Fund can be seen to operate as an instrument of redistribution, as a 'bribe' to maintain commitment to the integration process (Geyer 2000) it has also, while devolving managerial and administrative powers to Member States, steadily increased its powers as a proactive instrument of policy. Indeed, it is its flexibility and its essential redistributive function that has enabled it to develop into a more significant instrument of policy. From within the discourse of economic growth it has been a relatively weak instrument of VET policy and, for much of the time, an illusionary instrument of labour market policy. However, from within the discourse of political stability, it has, more significantly, unobtrusively operated as an instrument of European policy, directing, through its redistributive financial power, policy that is fundamentally more concerned with social and regional stability than with growth.

Appendix 1:
Key Legislation

CEC 1957	Treaty of the European Economic Community
CEC 1963	Common Vocational Training Policy
CEC 1971a,b	First reform of the ESF
CEC 1974a	Social action programme
CEC 1977a	Second reform of the ESF
CEC 1982a	Action to combat unemployment
CEC 1983a,d	Third reform of the ESF
CEC 1985a	Action to combat long-term unemployment
CEC 1986b	Single European Act
CEC 1988a	Fourth reform of the ESF
CEC 1988e	Combining the Structural Funds
CEC 1989a	Charter of Fundamental Social Rights
CEC 1992a	Treaty on the European Union
CEC 1993a	Fifth reform of the ESF
CEC 1993c	Reform of the Structural Funds
CEC 1996a	Mainstreaming equal opportunities
CEC 1997b	Amsterdam Treaty
CEC 1997c	Agenda 2000
CEC 1999a	Sixth reform of the ESF
CEC 1999b	Employment Guidelines
CEC 1999d	Reform of the Structural Funds

Appendix 2:
Legality of EU Policy Documents

Regulations supplement existing legislation and Member States must observe them in full and as stated; the compliance of Member States can be demanded. Regulations are extremely precise documents.

Directives also supplement existing legislation. The result to be achieved is binding on the Member States, but each Member State may choose the means by which they achieve the result. Directives can be less specific than Regulations.

Decisions are also binding in their entirety. They may refer to a specific area of policy, to all Member States or to selected Member States.

Opinions and *Recommendations* carry no legal force and hence are not binding on the Member States. They simply express the Commission's recommended action or opinion on a particular issue.

Appendix 3:
The Treaties and their Article Numbers

	Rome	SEA	TEU	Amsterdam
Unemployment	—	—	—	118
ESF	123	—	123	146
	124	—	124	147
	125	—	125	148
Education	—	—	126	149
Vocational training	128	—	127	150
Economic/social cohesion	—	130a	130a	158

Appendix 4:
Definition of Selected Terms Used within Regulation 1260/1999 on the Structural Funds (CEC 1999d)

Programming: the organizing, decision-making and financing process carried out in a number of stages to implement on a multi-annual basis the joint action of the Community and the Member States to attain the objectives referred to in Article 1 (p. 12).

Development plan: the analysis of the situation prepared by a Member State in the light of the objectives referred to in Article 1 and the priority needs for attaining those objectives, together with the strategy, the planned action priorities, their specific goals and the related indicative financial resources (p. 12).

Community Support Framework: the document approved by the Commission, in agreement with the Member State concerned, following appraisal of the plan submitted by a Member State and containing the strategy and priorities for action of the Funds and the Member States, their specific objectives, the contribution of the Funds and the other financial resources. This document shall be divided into priorities and implemented by means of one or more operational programmes (p. 12).

Operational programme: the document approved by the Commission to implement a Community Support Framework and comprising a consistent set of priorities comprising multi-annual measures and which may be implemented through recourse to one or more Funds, to one or more of the other existing financial instruments and to the EIB. An integrated operational programme means an operational programme financed by more than one Fund (p. 12).

Single Programming Document: a single document approved by the Commission and containing the same information to be found in a Community Support Framework and operational programme (p. 12).

Priority: one of the priorities of the strategy adopted in a Community Support Framework or assistance; to it is assigned a contribution from the Funds and other financial instruments and the relevant financial resources of the Member State and a set of specified targets (p. 12).

Additionality: In order to achieve a genuine economic impact, the appropriations of the Funds may not replace public or other equivalent structural expenditure by the Member State. For this purpose, the Commission and the Member State concerned shall determine the level of public or equivalent structural expenditure that the Member State is to maintain ... in advance of the Commission decision approving any Community Support Framework or single programming documents relating to the Member State concerned and shall be integrated into those documents (p. 14).

Bibliography

Amin, A., and J. Tommaney
    1995   *Behind the Myth of European Union: Prospects for Cohesion* (London: Routledge).

Anderson, J.
    1995   'Structural Funds and the Social Dimension of EU Policy: Springboard or Stumbling Block?' in S. Liebfried and P. Pierson (eds.), *European Social Policy: Between Fragmentation and Integration* (Washington DC: Brookings Institute): 123-58.

Arnot, M.
    1997   ' "Gendered Citizenry": New Feminist Perspectives on Education and Citizenship', *British Educational Research Journal*, 23.3: 275-95.

Atkinson, R., and S. Davoudi
    2000   'The Concept of Social Exclusion in the European Union: Context, Development and Possibilities', *Journal of Common Market Studies*, 38.3: 427-48.

Bache, I.
    1998   *The Regional and Structural Policies of the European Union* (Sheffield: Sheffield Academic Press).

Ball, S.J.
    1994   *Education Reform: A Critical and Post-structural Approach* (Buckingham: Open University Press).

Barnett, R.R., and V. Boorooah
    1995   'The Additionality (or otherwise) of European Community Structural Funds', in S. Hardy (ed.), *An Enlarged Europe: Regions or Competition?* (London: Jessica Kingsley Publications): 37-61.

Beck, W., L. van der Maesen and A. Walker (eds.)
    1998   *The Social Quality of Europe* (Bristol: Policy Press).

Brine, J.
    1992   'The European Social Fund and the Vocational Training of Unemployed Women: Questions of Gendering and Regendering', *Gender and Education* 4.1-2: 149-62.
    1995a   'Educational and Vocational Policy and the Construction of the European Union', *International Studies in the Education of Adults,* 5.2: 145-63.
    1995b   'Equal Opportunities and the European Social Fund: Discourse and Practice', *Gender and Education,* 7.1: 9-22.
    1997   'European Education and Training Policy for Under-educated Unemployed People, *International Studies in Sociology of Education,* 7.2: 229-45.

1998   'The European Union's Discourse of "Equality" and its Education and Training Policy within the Post-compulsory Sector', *Journal of Education Policy,* 13.1: 137-52.

1999a   'Economic Growth, Social Exclusion and the European Discourse of Equality: Pathologizing 'the Unemployed', *Research Papers in Education,* 14.1: 93-105.

1999b   *Under Educating Women: Globalizing Inequality* (Buckingham: Open University).

1999c   *The European Social Fund and the UK FE Sector* (University of Sheffield, Department of Educational Studies).

2000   'Mainstreaming European "Equal Opportunities": Marginalizing UK Training for Women', in J. Salisbury and S. Riddell (eds.), *Gender, Policy and Educational Change: Shifting Agendas in the UK and Europe* (London: Routledge).

2002   'FE Participation, European Expansion and European Erasure', *British Educational Research Journal* 28.1 (in press).

Burton, P., and R. Smith

1996   'The United Kingdom', in H. Heinelt and R. Smith (eds.), *Policy Networks and European Structural Funds* (Aldershot: Avebury): 74-81.

CEC (Commission of the European Communities)

1957   *Treaty Establishing the European Economic Community* (Brussels: European Commission).

1963   'Decision on a Common Vocational Training Policy (63/226/EEC) 10 April 1963', *Official Journal,* 63: 20.4.63.

1971a   'Council Decision of 1 February 1971 on the Reform of the European Social Fund (71/66/EEC)', *Official Journal,* L28: 4.2.71.

1971b   'Regulation (EEC) No 2396/71 of the Council of 8 November 1971 Implementing the Council Decision of 1 February 1971 on the Reform of the European Social Fund', *Official Journal,* L 249: 10.11.71: 924-28.

1971c   'Regulation (EEC) No 2397/71 of the Council of 8 November 1971 on Aid which May Qualify for Assistance from the European Social Fund', *Official Journal,* L 249: 10.11.71: 919-31.

1971d   'Regulation (EEC) No 2398/71 of the Council of 8 November 1971 on Assistance from the European Social Fund for Persons who Are to Pursue Activities in a Self-employed Capacity', *Official Journal,* L 249: 10.11.71: 932.

1972a   'Council Decision of 19 December 1972 on Assistance from the European Social Fund for Persons Leaving Agriculture to Pursue Non-agricultural Activities (72/428/EEC)', *Official Journal,* L 291: 28.12.72: 73-74.

1972b   'Council Decision of 19 December 1972 on Intervention by the European Social Fund in Favour of Persons Occupied in the Textile Industry (72/429/EEC)', *Official Journal,* L 291: 28.12.72: 75-76.

1972c   'Regulation (EEC) No 858/72 of the Council of 24 April 1972 on Certain Administrative and Financial Procedures for the Operation of the European Social Fund', *Official Journal,* L 101: 28.4.72: 353-55.

1973a 'Regulation (EEC/2005/73) of the Commission of 25 July 1973 on the Fixing of a Maximum Amount of Assistance from the European Social Fund for Certain Types of Aid', *Official Journal,* L 205: 26.7.73: 13.

1973b 'Commission Decision (73/434/EEC) of 28 November 1973 on the Submission of Applications for Assistance from the European Social Fund', *Official Journal,* L 355: 24.12.73: 68.

1974a 'Council Resolution of 21 January 1974 Concerning a Social Action Programme', *Official Journal,* C 13: 12.2.74: 1-4.

1974b 'Council Directive of 18 February 1974 on Stability, Growth and Full Employment in the Community (74/121/EEC)', *Official Journal,* L 63: 19-20.

1974c 'Council Decision 74/328/EEC of 27 June 1974 on Action by the European Social Fund for Handicapped Persons', *Official Journal,* L 185: 9.7.74: 22-23.

1974d 'Regulation EEC/1761/74 of the Council of 27 June 1974 Amending Council Regulation EEC/2397/71 on Aid which May Qualify for Assistance from the European Social Fund', *Official Journal,* L 185: 9/7/74: 1.

1975a 'Council Decision 75/459/EEC of 22 July 1975 on Action by the European Social Fund for Persons Affected by Employment Difficulties', *Official Journal,* L 199: 30.7.75: 36.

1975b 'Council Regulation EEC/337/75 of 10 February Establishing a European Centre for the Development of Vocational Training', *Official Journal,* L 39: 13.2.75: 1-4.

1975c 'Council Decision 75/458/EEC of 22 July 1975 Concerning a Programme of Pilot Schemes and Studies to Combat Poverty', *Official Journal,* L 199: 30.7.75: 34-35.

1976a 'Council Resolution of 9 February 1976 Comprising an Action Programme in the Field of Education', *Official Journal,* C 38: 19.2.76: 1-5.

1976b 'Council Resolution of 13 December Concerning Measures to Be Taken to Improve the Preparation of Young People for Work and to Facilitate their Transition from Education to Working Life', *Official Journal,* C 308: 30.12.76: 1-3.

1976c 'Council Decision 76/206/EEC of 9 February 1976 on Intervention by the European Social Fund in Favour of Persons Occupied in the Textile and Clothing Industries', *Official Journal,* L 39: 14.2.76: 39.

1976d 'Council Directive 76/207/EEC of 9 February 1976 on the Implementation of the Principle of Equal Treatment for Men and Women as Regards Access to Employment, Vocational Training and Promotion and Working Conditions', *Official Journal,* L 39: 14.2.76: 40-42.

1977a 'Council Regulation EEC/2893/77 of 20 December 1977 amending Regulation EEC/2396/71 Implementing the Council Decision of 1 February 1971 on the Reform of the European Social Fund', *Official Journal,* L 337: 27.12.77: 1-6.

1977b 'Commission Recommendation (77/467/EEC) of 6 July 1977 to the Member States on Vocational Preparation for Young People who Are Unemployed or threatened by Unemployment', *Official Journal,* L 180: 20.7.77: 18-23.

1977c   'Council Regulation EEC/2895/77 of 20 December 1977 Concerning Operations Qualifying for a Higher Rate of Intervention by the European Social Fund', *Official Journal*, L 337: 27.12.77: 7.

1977d   'Council Decision 77/801/EEC of 20 December 1977 Amending Decision 71/66/EEC on the Reform of the European Social Fund', *Official Journal*, L 337: 27.12.77: 8-9.

1977e   'Council Decision 77/802/EEC of 20 December 1977 Amending Certain Decisions Adopted Pursuant to Article 4 of Decision 71/66/EEC on the Reform of the European Social Fund', *Official Journal*, L 337: 10-11.

1977f   'Council Decision 77/803/EEC of 20 December 1977 on Action by the European Social Fund for Migrant Workers', *Official Journal*, L 337: 27.12.77: 12-13.

1977g   'Council Decision 77/804/EEC of 20 December 1977 on Action by the European Social Fund for Women', *Official Journal*, L 337: 27.12.77: 14.

1978a   'Commission Decision 78/706/EEC of 27 July 1978 on Certain Administrative Procedures for the Operation of the European Social Fund', *Official Journal*, L 238: 30.8.78: 20-21.

1978b   'Council Regulation EEC/3039/78 of 18 December 1978 on the Creation of Two New Types of Aid for Young People from the European Social Fund', *Official Journal*, L 361: 23.12.78: 3-4.

1980a   'Council Resolution of 27 June 1980 on Guidelines for a Community Labour Market Policy', *Official Journal*, C 168: 8.7.80: 1-4.

1981a   'Women and the European Social Fund', *Women of Europe Supplement*, 81, 6.

1982a   'Council Resolution of 12 July 1982 on Community Action to Combat Unemployment', *Official Journal*, C 186: 21.7.82: 1-2.

1982b   'Council Resolution of 12 July 1982 on the Promotion of Equal Opportunities for Women (First Medium-term Community Action Programme 1982-1985)', *Official Journal*, C 186: 21.7.82: 3-4.

1982c   'Resolution of the Council of 12 July Concerning Measures to Be Taken to Improve the Preparation of Young People for Work and to Facilitate their Transition from Education to Working Life', *Official Journal*, C 193: 28.7.82: 1-2.

1983a   'Council Regulation EEC/2950/83 of 17 October 1983 on the Implementation of Decision 83/516/EEC on the Tasks of the European Social Fund', *Official Journal*, L 289: 22.10.83: 1-3.

1983b   'The Solemn Declaration of Stuttgart on European Union 19 June 1983', *Bulletin of the European Communities*, 6: 24-29.

1983c   'Council Resolution of 2 June Concerning Vocational Training Measures Relating to New Information Technologies', *Official Journal*, C 166: 25.6.83: 1-3.

1983d   'Council Decision 83/516/EEC of 17 October 1983 on the Tasks of the European Social Fund', *Official Journal*, L 289: 22.10.83: 38-40.

1984a   'Council Recommendation 84/635/EEC of 13 December 1984 on the Promotion of Positive Action for Women', *Official Journal*, L 331:19.12.84: 34-35.

1985a   'Council Resolution 85/C 2/03 of 19 December 1984 on Action to Combat Long-term Unemployment', *Official Journal*, C 2: 4.1.85: 3-5.

1985b   'Council Decision 85/8/EEC of 19 December 1984 on Specific Community Action to Combat Poverty', *Official Journal*, L 2: 3.1.85: 24-25.

1985c   *Completing the Internal Market*, White Paper from the Commission to the European Communities (Milan 28–29 June 1985) (COM(85)0310 FINAL).

1985d   'New Technologies and Social Change: Office Automation', *Social Europe Supplement* (Luxembourg: Office for Official Publications of the European Communities).

1985e   'Council Decision 85/368/EEC of 16 July on the Comparability of Vocational Training Qualifications between the Member States of the European Community', *Official Journal*, L 199: 31.7.85: 56-59.

1985f   'Equal Opportunities for Women: Second Medium-term Community Programme (1986-1990) (COM(85)801 FINAL)', *Official Journal*, C 356: 31.12.85: 28.

1985g   'Council Regulation EEC 3824/85 of 20 December 1985 Amending, with a View to its Extension to Cover Self-employed Persons, Regulation EEC 2950/83 on the Implementation of Decision 83/516/EEC on the Tasks of the European Social Fund', *Official Journal*, L 370: 31.12.85: 25.

1986a   'Where Will the New Jobs Be? Sectoral and Occupational Employment Prospects in some Industrialized Countries up to the Year 2000', *Social Europe*, 3: 23-37.

1986b   'Single European Act', *Bulletin of the European Communities*, 86.2: 1-24.

1987a   *New Forms and New Areas of Employment Growth: A Comparative Study* (Luxembourg: Office for Official Publications of the European Communities).

1987b   'Council Decision 87/569/EEC of 1 December Concerning an Action Programme for the Vocational Training of Young People and their Preparation for Adult and Working Life', *Official Journal*, L 346: 10.12.87: 31-33.

1988a   'Council Regulation EEC/4255/88 of 19 December 1988 Laying Down Provisions for Implementing Regulation (EEC) No 2052/88 as Regards the European Social Fund', *Official Journal*, L 374: 31.12.88:21-24.

1988b   'The Hanover Council of 27–28 June 1988', *Bulletin of the European Communities*, 88.6: 164-67.

1988c   'Council Resolution 88/C 177/02 of 24 May 1988 on the European Dimension in Education', *Official Journal*, C 177: 6.7.88: 5-7.

1988d   'Council Decision 88/348/EEC of 16 June 1988 Adopting an Action Programme for the Promotion of Youth Exchanges in the Community – "Youth for Europe" Programme', *Official Journal*, L 158: 25.6.88: 42-46.

1988e   'Council Regulation 2052/88 of 24 June 1988 on the Tasks of the Structural Funds and their Effectiveness and on Coordination of their Activities between Themselves and with the Operations of the European Investment Bank and the other Existing Financial Instruments', *Official Journal*, L 185: 15.7.88: 9-19.

1989a   *Community Charter of Fundamental Social Rights of Workers* (COM(89)471 FINAL).

1989b   'Council Resolution 89/C 277/01 of 29 September 1989 on Combating Social Exclusion', *Official Journal,* C 277: 31.10.89: 1.

1989c   'Guidelines Concerning European Social Fund Intervention in respect of Action against Long-term Unemployment and Occupational Integration of Young People (Objectives 3 and 4 in the Context of the Reform of the Structural Funds)', *Official Journal,* C 45: 24.2.89: 6-9.

1989d   'Council Decision 89/457/EEC of 18 July 1989 Establishing a Medium-term Community Action Programme Concerning the Economic and Social Integration of the Economically and Socially Less Privileged Groups in Society', *Official Journal,* L 224: 2.8.89: 10-14.

1991a   'Council Resolution of 21 May 1991 on the Third Medium-term Community Action Programme on Equal Opportunities for Women and Men (1991–1995)', *Official Journal,* C 142: 31.5.91: 1-3.

1991b   'Council Decision 91/387/EEC of 22 July 1991 Amending Decision 87/569/EEC Concerning an Action Programme for the Vocational Training of Young People and their Preparation for Adult and Working Life (Petra)', *Official Journal,* L 214: 2.8.91: 69-76.

1991c   'Council Decision 91/395/EEC of 29 July 1991 Adopting the "Youth for Europe" Programme (second phase)', *Official Journal,* L 217: 6.8.91: 25-30.

1992a   *Treaty on European Union* (Luxembourg: Office for Official Publications of the European Communities).

1992b   'Council Resolution 93/C 49/02 of 21 December 1992 on the Need to Tackle the Serious and Deteriorating Situation Concerning Unemployment in the Community', *Official Journal,* C 49: 19.2.93: 3-6.

1993a   'Council Regulation 2084/93/EEC of 20 July 1993 Amending Regulation EEC/4255/88 Laying Down Provisions for Implementing Regulation EEC/2052/88 as Regards the European Social Fund', *Official Journal,* L 193: 31.7.93: 39-43.

1993b   *White Paper: Growth, Competitiveness, Employment: The Challenges and Ways Forward into the 21st Century* (Luxembourg: Office for Official Publications of the European Communities).

1993c   'Council Regulation (EEC) 2081/93 of 20 July 1993 Amending Regulation (EEC) No 2052/88 on the Tasks of the Structural Funds and their Effectiveness and on Coordination of their Activities between Themselves and with the Operations of the European Investment Bank and the other Exiting Financial Instruments', *Official Journal,* L 193: 31.7.93: 5-19.

1994a   *European Social Policy: A Way Forward for the Union - A White Paper (COM(94)333) 27 July 1994* (Luxembourg: Office for Official Publications of the European Communities).

1994b   'Council Resolution 94/C 231/01 of 22 June 1994 on the Promotion of Equal Opportunities for Women and Men through Action by the European Structural Funds', *Official Journal,* C 231: 20.8.94:1-2.

1994c   'Council Decision 94/819/EC of 6 December Establishing an Action Programme for the Implementation of a European Community Vocational Training Policy "Leonardo da Vinci"', *Official Journal*, L 340: 29.12.94: 8-24.

1995a   *White Paper: Education and Training: Teaching and Learning: Towards the Learning Society (COM(95)590)* (Luxembourg: Office for Official Publications of the European Communities).

1995b   'Council Decision of 22 December 1995 on a Medium-term Community Action Programme on Equal Opportunities for Men and Women (1996-2000)', *Official Journal*, L 335: 30.12.95: 37-41.

1996a   'Council Resolution 96/C 386/01 of 2 December 1996 on Mainstreaming Equal Opportunities for Men and Women into the European Structural Funds', *Official Journal*, C 386: 20.12.96: 1-3.

1996b   'Action for Employment in Europe: A Confidence Pact', *Bulletin of the European Communities*, 96.4: 1-33.

1997a   'Special Luxembourg European Council on Employment', *Bulletin of the European Communities*, 97.11: 7-13.

1997b   'Treaty of Amsterdam Amending the Treaty on European Union, the Treaties Establishing the European Communities and Certain Related Acts', *Official Journal*, 97: 1-144.

1997c   'Agenda 2000: For a Stronger and Wider Union', *Bulletin of the European Communities*, 97.5: 1-80.

1999a   'Regulation (EC) No 1784/1999 of the European Parliament and of the Council of 12 July 1999 on the European Social Fund', *Official Journal*, L213: 13.8.99: 5-8.

1999b   *The 1999 Employment Guidelines: Council Resolution of 22 February 1999* (Luxembourg: Office for Official Publications of the European Communities).

1999c   'Presidency Conclusions: Berlin European Council 24 and 25 March 1999 (SN 100/99)', http://europa.eu.int/council/off/concl/mar99_en.pdf

1999d   'Council Regulation (EC) 1260/1999 Laying Down General Provisions on the Structural Funds', *Official Journal*, L 161: 26.6.1999: 1.

2000a   'Presidency Conclusions: Lisbon European Council, 23 and 24 March 2000', http://europa.eu.int/council/off/concl/mar00_en.pdf

2000b   *White Paper Presenting Proposals for the Reform of the Commission* (Luxembourg: Office for Official Publications of the European Communities).

2000c   *Treaty of Nice.*

Collins, D.
1975   *The European Communities: The Social Policy of the First Phase. The European Economic Community 1958–72 Vol. 2* (London: Martin Robertson & Co.).

1983   *The Operation of the European Social Fund* (London: Croom Helm).

Corbett, A.
1998   'Explaining Erasmus: A Historical Institutionalist Approach to Researching EU Education Policy' (paper presented to UACES Research Conference, University of Lincoln).

Council of Europe
    1973   *The Educational Needs of the 16–19 Age Group: The Janne Report* (Strasbourg: Council of Europe).

Cram, L.
    1997   *Policy-making in the European Union* (London: Routledge).

Dinan, D.
    1999a   *Ever Closer Union: An Introduction to the European Community* (Basingstoke: Macmillan).
    1999b   'Governance and Institutions: A Transitional Year', in G. Edwards and G. Wiessala (eds.), *The European Union: Annual Review 1998/1999* (Oxford: Basil Blackwell): 37-61.

Falkner, G.
    1998   'Enlarging the European Union', in J. Richardson (ed.), *European Union: Power and Policy-making* (London: Routledge): 233-46.

Field, J.
    1994   *Educational and Vocational Training Policy* (Harlow: Longman).
    1998   *European Dimensions: Education, Training and the European Union* (London: Jessica Kingsley).

Fiske, J.
    1995   *Media Matters: Everyday Culture and Political Change* (Minneapolis, MN: Minnesota University Press).

Foucault, M.
    1980   *The Will to Knowledge: The History of Sexuality, Vol. 1* (Harmondsworth: Penguin Books).

Galloway, D.
    1999   'Agenda 2000: Packaging the Deal', in G. Edwards and G. Wiessala (eds.), *The European Union: Annual Review 1998/1999* (Oxford: Basil Blackwell): 9-35.

Geyer, R.
    2000   *Exploring European Social Policy* (Cambridge: Polity).

George, S.
    1996   *Politics and Policy in the European Union* (Oxford: Oxford University Press).

Hantrais, L.
    1995   *Social Policy in the European Union* (London: Macmillan).

Harrop, J.
    1996   *Structural Funding and Employment in the European Union: Financing the Path to Integration* (Cheltenham: Edward Elgar).

Harryvan, A., and J. van der Harst
    1997   *Documents on European Union* (London: Macmillan).

Heinelt, H., and R. Smith (eds.)
    1996   *Policy Networks and the European Structural Funds* (Aldershot: Avebury).

Henriques, J.
    1984   *Changing the Subject: Psychology, Social Regulation and Subjectivity* (London: Methuen).

Hine, D., and H. Kassim (eds.)
    1998   *Beyond the Market: The EU and National Social Policy* (London: Routledge).

Howarth, D.
    2000   *Discourse* (Buckingham: Open University Press).

Jackman, R.
    1998   'The Impact of the European Union on Unemployment and Unemployment Policy', in Hine and Kassim (1998): 60-78.

Keating, M., and L. Hooghe
    1996   'By-passing the Nation State? Regions and the EU Policy Process', in J. Richardson (ed.), *European Union: Power and Policy-making* (London: Routledge): 216-29.

Kendall, G., and G. Wickham
    1999   *Using Foucault's Methods* (London: Sage).

Kohli, J.
    1998   ' "Race": An Emergent Policy Area in the European Union', in R. Sykes and P. Alcock (eds.), *Developments in European Social Policy: Convergence and Diversity* (Bristol: Policy Press): 171-89.

Laffan, B.
    1983   'Policy Implementation in the European Community: The European Social Fund as a Case Study', *Journal of Common Market Studies,* 21.4: 389-408.

Levitas, R.
    1998   *The Inclusive Society? Social Exclusion and New Labour* (London: Macmillan).

Liebfried, S., and P. Pierson (eds.)
    1995   *European Social Policy: Between Fragmentation and Integration* (Washington, DC: The Brookings Institution).

Lindstrom, C.
    2000   'Lifelong Learning at European Level: The Past, the Present and the New Grundtvig Action', *Lifelong Learning in Europe,* 4.1: 31-34.

Littlewood, P., I. Glorieux, S. Herkommer and I. Jonsson
    1999   *Social Exclusion in Europe: Problems and Paradigms* (Aldershot: Ashgate).

Macmillen, M.
    1982   'European Social Fund Aid to Migrants', *Social Policy and Administration,* 16.1: 63-78.

Mazey, S.
    1998   'The European Union and Women's Rights: From the Europeanisation of National Agendas to the Nationalisation of a European Agenda?' in Hine and Kassim (1998): 134-55.

McAllister, R.
    1997   *From EC to EU: An Historical and Political Survey* (London: Routledge).

McDonald, M.
    1997   'Identities in the European Commission', in N. Nugent (ed.), *At the Heart of the Union: Studies of the European Commission* (London: Macmillan): 49-69.

Middlemas, K.
     1995   *Orchestrating Europe: The Informal Politics of the European Union 1973–1995* (London: Fontana Press).
Milner, S.
     1998   'EC Training Policy', *European Business and Economic Development,* 1.1: 15-22.
Moravcsik, A., and K. Nicolaidis
     1999   'Explaining the Treaty of Amsterdam: Interests, Influence, Institutions', *Journal of Common Market Studies,* 37.1: 59-85.
Moreton, T.
     1992   'European Support for People with Disabilities', *Personnel Review,* 21.6: 74-87.
Nugent, N.
     1999   *The Government and Politics of the European Community* (Basingstoke: Macmillan).
Osler, A.
     1998   'European Citizenship and Study Abroad: Student Teachers' Experiences and Identities', *Cambridge Journal of Education,* 28.1: 77-96.
Ozga, J.
     2000   *Policy Research in Educational Settings* (Buckingham: Open University Press).
Peterson, J.
     1997   'Decision-making in the European Union: Towards a Framework for Analysis', in N. Nugent (ed.), *The European Union: Volume 1* (Aldershot: Dartmouth Publishing): 79-103.
Pochet, P.
     1999   'The New Employment Chapter of the Amsterdam Treaty', *Journal of European Social Policy* 9.3: 271-78.
Prechal, S., and L. Senden
     1993   *Equal Treatment after Maastricht: Special Report of 1993 of the Network of Experts on the Implementation of the Equality Directives* (Brussels: European Commission, DG V, Equal Opportunities Unit).
Rees, T.
     1995   'Women and Training Policy in the European Union', *Gender, Work and Organization,* 2.2: 34-45.
     1998   *Mainstreaming Equality in the European Union* (London: Routledge).
Richardson, J. (ed.)
     1996   *European Union: Power and Policy-making* (London: Routledge).
Rowan, D.
     1998   'Meet the New World Government', *The Guardian,* 13 February.
Springer, B.
     1992   *The Social Dimension of 1992: Europe Faces a New EC* (New York: Greenwood Press).
Staeck, N.
     1996   'The European Structural Funds: Their History and Impact' in H. Heinelt (ed.), *Policy Networks and European Structural Funds* (Aldershot: Avebury): 46-72.

Swann, D.
    1992   *The Single European Market and Beyond: A Study of the Wider Implications of the Single European Act* (London: Routledge).

Sykes, R., and P. Alcock (eds.)
    1998   *Developments in European Social Policy: Convergence or Diversity?* (Bristol: Policy Press).

Taylor, P.
    1983   *The Limits of European Integration* (Columbia: Columbia University Press).

Teichler, U., and F. Maiworm
    1994   *Transition to Work: The Experiences of Former ERASMUS Students* (London: Jessica Kingsley).

Titscher, S., M. Meyer, R. Wodak and E. Vetter
    2000   *Methods of Text and Discourse Analysis* (London: Sage).

Urwin, D.
    1995   *The Community of Europe: A History of European Integration since 1945* (Harlow: Addison Wesley Longman).

Wallace, H., and W. Wallace
    1996   *Policy-making in the European Union* (Oxford: Oxford University Press).

General Index

Index of Authors

UNIVERSITY ASSOCIATION FOR CONTEMPORARY EUROPEAN STUDIES
UACES Secretariat, King's College London, Strand, London WC2R 2LS, UK
Tel: +44 (0)20 7240 0206   Fax: +44 (0)20 7836 2350   Email: admin@uaces.org
www.uaces.org

UACES

University Association for Contemporary European Studies

The Association
- Brings together academics involved in researching Europe with representatives of government, industry and the media who are active in European affairs
- Primary organisation for British academics researching the European Union
- Over 600 individual and corporate members from Dept such as Politics, Law, Economics & European Studies, plus over 150 Graduate Students who join as Associate Members

Membership Benefits
- Individual Members eligible for special highly reduced fee for The Journal of Common Market Studies (JCMS)
- Regular Newsletter - events and developments of relevance to members
- Conferences - variety of themes, modestly priced, further reductions for members
- Publications, including the new series *Contemporary European Studies*, launched in 1998
- Research Network, and research conference
- Through the European Community Studies Association (ECSA), access to a larger world wide network
- Information Documentation & Resources eg: The Register of Courses in European Studies and the Register of Research into European Integration

Current Cost of Membership per annum
Individual Members: £25.00   Associate (Student): £10.00   Corporate Members: £50.00

APPLICATION FOR MEMBERSHIP OF UACES
Please complete the appropriate details and return the entire form to the address above.

Last Name: _____ First Name: _____ Title (eg Mr): ____

Institution: _____

Faculty / Dept: _____

Institution Address: _____

_____

Work Tel No: _____   Work Fax No: _____

Home Tel No: _____   Home Fax No: _____

E-mail: _____

Address for correspondence if different: _____

_____

Where did you hear about UACES? _____

Signature and Date: _____

PTO TO COMPLETE PAYMENT DETAILS

UNIVERSITY ASSOCIATION FOR CONTEMPORARY EUROPEAN STUDIES
UACES Secretariat, King's College London, Strand, London WC2R 2LS, UK
Tel: +44 (0)20 7240 0206   Fax: +44 (0)20 7836 2350   Email: admin@uaces.org
www.uaces.org

PAYMENT DETAILS

TO PAY BY CHEQUE*

I wish to pay my membership subscription by cheque. Please make cheques payable to UACES, not King's College.

Please find enclosed a cheque (in pounds sterling) for:
   £25 (Individual)   £10 (Associate - Student)   £50 (Corporate)

* Please Note: we are no longer able to accept Eurocheques

TO PAY BY CREDIT/DEBIT CARD

I wish to pay my membership subscription by (mark appropriate box):
   Visa   Mastercard   Eurocard   Switch Solo

I authorise you to debit my Account with the amount of (mark appropriate box):
   £25 (Individual)   £10 (Associate - Student)   £50 (Corporate)

Signature of cardholder: _____   Date: _____

My Card Number is: ☐☐☐☐   ☐☐☐☐   ☐☐☐☐   ☐☐☐☐   ☐☐☐

Cardholder's Name and Initials*:_____ Cardholder's Title* (eg Mr): _____
*As shown on the card

Expiry Date: ☐☐☐   Start Date (if present*): ☐☐☐   Issue No. (if present*): ☐
*Usually for Switch and Solo cards

Cardholder's address and postcode (if different from overleaf):
_____

TO PAY BY STANDING ORDER* (UK Bank only)
*This option not available for Corporate or Associate (Student) members

Please complete the details below and return to UACES. We will process the membership application and then forward this authority to your bank. This authority is not a Direct Debit authority (ie we cannot take money out of your bank account without your permission).

To (insert your Bank Name) _____ at (insert your bank address)
_____
_____ (insert Post Code) _____, UK.

Please pay to Lloyds Bank, Pall Mall Branch, 8-10 Waterloo Place, London SW1Y 4BE, UK, in favour of UACES, Account No. 3781242, Sort-Code 30-00-08, on the (insert date, eg 1st) _____ day of (insert month, eg June) _____ , the sum of £25 (TWENTY FIVE POUNDS) and the same sum on the same date each year until countermanded.

Signature: _____   Date: _____
Name: _____
Address: _____
Account No.: _____   Sort-code: _____

CES Ad1